Anthology
2016

COVINGTON WRITERS GROUP

COVINGTON WRITERS GROUP
ANTHOLOGY 2016

Elle Mott, Managing Editor
Jenny Breeden, Executive Editor
Gary Reed and Mikey Chlanda, Proofreaders

ISBN: 1945368047
ISBN-13: 978-1945368042

PUBLISHED BY COVINGTON WRITERS GROUP, INC.
IN CONJUNCTION WITH
SEAGULL PRODUCTIONS LLC
COVINGTON, KY 41014

ANTHOLOGY 2016

DISCLAIMERS

TABLE OF CONTENTS

ACKNOWLEDGEMENTS ix

INTRODUCTION 1

POETRY 3

IS IT A POEM? 5
   by Gary Reed
WOOING CONTEST 5
   by Gary Reed
FRUSTRATION 6
   by Patti Kay Emerson
MY ALMOST BROTHER 7
   by Alvena Stanfield
MESSAGE FROM HEAVEN 8
   by Patti Kay Emerson
THE LONG-TAILED PANGOLIN 9
   by Gary Reed
MAUDLIN PANGOLIN 9
   by Gary Reed
HE IS, HE IS 10
   by Elle Mott
SHE IS, SHE IS 12
   by Brad Hudepohl
GRIEF 13
   by Patti Kay Emerson
SEASONS 14
   by Jenny Breeden
PATIENCE 16
   by Patti Kay Emerson
CHINESE BUFFET 17
   by Gary Reed

TRAIN TO NOWHERE 18
by Patti Kay Emerson
FLYING SOLO 19
by Liz Shipwash

STORIES 21

POMP AS A BOY 23
by Brad Hudepohl
FRONTIER MESSENGER 24
Chapter 1: Foundlings
by Alvena Stanfield
BURNING REVENGE 31
by Mikey Chlanda
MY COMMENCEMENT: A Memoir 38
by Elle Mott
MAYHEM AND A BEER CHASER 44
by L. N. Passmore
THE BRIDGE 52
by Jenny Breeden
PARENTS ARE THE BEST TEACHERS 82
by Alvena Stanfield
DAMSELS IN DISTRESS 84
by Leslie Bush
IT JUST DRIVES ME CRAZY 122
by Gary Reed
WORKING 9/11: A Firefighter's Perspective 141
by Mikey Chlanda
MY TOWER TO FREEDOM: A Memoir 146
by Elle Mott
HOW BRIGHT EYE BECAME SKY-WULF 152
by L. N. Passmore
ALL WILL BE OKAY 158
by Alvena Stanfield

DOUBLECROSS: A Shaeffer Novel 161
   by Mikey Chlanda

ABOUT THE AUTHORS 165

Jenny Breeden 167

Leslie Bush 168

Mikey Chlanda 169

Patti Kay Emerson 170

Brad Hudepohl 171

Elle Mott 172

L. N. Passmore 173

Gary Reed 174

Alvena Stanfield 175

Liz Shipwash 176

CONTACT US 177

OTHER BOOKS 179

By Covington Writers Group

ACKNOWLEDGMENTS

The Covington Writers Group thanks our supporters:

John Graham and the staff at the Kenton County Public Library in Covington for providing a comfortable, state-of-the-art facility for our first and third Saturday morning meetings each month through September.

The staff at Zola Pub and Grill in MainStrasse Village in Covington for providing us with their spacious second floor dining area on the second and fourth Saturday evenings each month, so we can relax, socialize and critique stories.

Roebling Point Books and Coffee in Covington for providing a friendly alternative meeting place whenever we needed one and for offering our books for sale.

Left Bank Coffeehouse in Covington for providing coffee services for some of our meetings, seminars and special presentations.

The Center for Great Neighborhoods (CGN) in Covington for welcoming us into their new community building in October for our first and third Saturday morning meetings each month. Eager to partner with small creative businesses, the CGN is a catalyst for positive growth, an exciting opportunity for our group.

The Covington Coffee Company in Covington for providing a relaxing neighborhood environment and a great cup of coffee and for agreeing to be our new coffee connection before and during meetings and for our future seminars and presentations.

INTRODUCTION

2016 was our third year as an active group. We offered a "Writing Romance Workshop" at a March meeting, presented by a former member, Michele Wyan. As a published romance author, she shared her insights and experiences with the romance writing industry. Our "Getting Published" seminar in May was free and open to the community. Member Jenny Breeden presented information on how to self-publish a book inexpensively and member Mikey Chlanda shared tips and tricks for building an author platform and marketing the book. In September, we published *Our Traditions*, a collection of personal narrative stories from our members with recipes and craft ideas. Most recently, we participated in the "First Annual Indie Author Day" which was sponsored locally by the Main Branch of the Boone County Public Library.

During the year, our poems and stories have been peer-reviewed by our members to strengthen our writing. It is a diverse collection from many genres, some enriched with our local area's history. We hope you enjoy our third annual anthology.

The members of Covington Writers Group express their heartfelt thanks to our families and friends for allowing us to spend some of our time away from them while we write, share our work at group meetings, and grow as writers. Their love and sacrifices mean the world to us as we strive for success.

POETRY

IS IT A POEM?
by Gary Reed

Is it a poem,
Really, if I'm
Just able to rhyme
Some of the time?

Is it a poem,
Truly, if I'm
Unable to rhyme,
Not even a line?

WOOING CONTEST
by Gary Reed

If I could enlist
My best poem in
A wooing contest,
Would I win
Her deepest affection
Or just pin
Honorable Mention?

FRUSTRATION
by Patti Kay Emerson

Some people think frustration means the end
But I know it could be the beginning
Of many wonderful things to come
If you use frustration in the right way
You may find it to be
A learning experience
Which can lead to creativity
And something new
Can come to be
Such as writing a poem
About frustration
To show that
Frustration does not mean
The end, but only a
New beginning to be born.

MY ALMOST BROTHER
by Alvena Stanfield

He was there months before me
Our mothers, best friends
We, apartment dwellers all
He, impulsive, daring, courageous
I, always following
Hand in hand
Wherever he led.
Violets along the riverbank
Our mothers' favorites
Called to us
In our fourth spring.
Discovered, almost there.
He, forced to choose the branch
We suffered wicked switching
I, slower, more than he.
Bruised streaks on our legs
Compelled him
To promise
Like the raven,
"Nevermore."
Impulse, daring and courage
Easily crushed before five.

MESSAGE FROM HEAVEN
by Patti Kay Emerson

I've been told that cardinals, pennies, and four leaf clovers
Are messages from our loved ones in Heaven.
If this is true, then he has been talking to me
The past three weeks
For I have seen a cardinal thrice,
Found a penny twice,
And picked a four-leaf clover once.
Today is his first birthday in Heaven.
"Who?" you may ask.
My best friend
And brother,
Charlie is his name
I miss him as much today
As the day he left.
Oh how I wish I could visit him today
But, alas heaven has no visiting hours.
However, if it's true the birds, pennies, and clovers
Are a message from him
I know he sees me today and that's enough for me.

In Memory of Charles Ray Emerson 6/18/1945 – 7/25/2015

THE LONG-TAILED PANGOLIN
by Gary Reed

The long-tailed pangolin,
A much-trafficked mammal,
Has scales made of keratin,
Is mainly nocturnal,
And sleeps rolled in a ball.

Like a skunk in funk, when
In danger, the pangolin –
Solitary, moody, anal –
Butt sprays a foul chemical.

MAUDLIN PANGOLIN
by Gary Reed

The little brown pangolin
Played a wicked mandolin
And crooned maudlin
Country-Western ballads
For the hard-working lads
Who frack gas and oil in
The North Dakota Bakken.

HE IS, HE IS
by Elle Mott

A man I never knew, void from my memory flashes,
When a woman called me to ask,
"Do you want me to send you his ashes?"

He was cast out of my life,
Because I was taken by my mother, his wife,

She, who called me, tells me we lived mountains aside,
And that he loved me dearly with no want to hide,

I wish I could have known him, if only he had known me,
Because with his passing life,
all that is left is his ashes to be forever free,

My address, I tell her,
When a week later I get his personal effects, which sets my heart astir,

I gaze upon his trinkets, tie-tacks, and medallions,
Because I feel him when I touch the
symbolic blue stones, golden amulets, and Texan stallions,

To steal away his bronze coin for me to find, in my pocket daily,
I wondered if he'd mind, for me to feel his love bravely,

He allows me, I believe, into his inner self as an open clue,
Because only now is his wisdom deep in me
as I come to love the man I never knew,

Now that his life is over, the stars will be grateful to have his ashy
dust,
Because only then can a shooting star release another soul,
as my father's soul is forever put to rest,

He is, he is.

Dedicated to Robert Frank "Bob" Wells (1943-2015),
Commanding Officer, U.S.N.R. (Ret. 1969)

SHE IS, SHE IS
by Brad Hudepohl

A woman of virtuous character is she,
When I express my tribulations, she listens to me,

She takes the darkness out of my life,
Because in her soul is light,

She lifts my spirit to the highest mountaintop,
And I wish our time together will never stop,

I wish I knew her better, if only I could,
Because she brings into my life, all that is lasting and good,

The caring person, which is her,
When I am with her, my heart is astir,

I gaze upon her eyes and see her gleam,
Because the sweetness of her touch is what I dream,

To steal a kiss from her lips, so tender,
Would be etched in my mind, always to remember,

She allows me to share my inner emotions,
Because her wisdom is as deep as the deepest oceans,

When her life is over, God will reward her,
Because of the loving kindness, that is inside her,

She is, she is.

GRIEF
by Patti Kay Emerson

Grief is a tricky emotion.
Some people think it should end at a certain time.
But grief does not work on a schedule.

It has its own sense of time
That is like no other.

For some people, grief lasts maybe a week
Or a month and they are back to
Their usual routine.

But for others, it may last years or
Even the rest of their lives.

For some people, each new loss
Brings back the grief from previous losses
And the process starts over again.

For some, the day or the month of their loss
Begins the grief over again each year.

I know about this because I am one of those people.
If I could fast-forward past February, I would do it in a minute
But since I can't, I must learn to live
With it all over again.

And each time I have a new loss,
No matter what the month,
It's February all over again.

SEASONS
by Jenny Breeden

Hot
Summer
Relaxing
In the cool shade
Hearing the birds sing
Sipping on lemonade
Fireworks light up the sky
Cookouts with friends and family
Hot dogs, watermelon, apple pie
We are so proud to be Americans

Cool
Autumn
Clean, crisp air
Fun times for all
Pumpkin patches, Halloween
Ice hockey and football
Needing a sweater at night
Time to honor our veterans
Taking chilly walks in the moonlight
Perfect chance to stargaze and be thankful

Cold
Winter
Snow and ice
Gets dark early
Warm hats, coats, and boots
Visits with family
Happy holidays to you
Sipping cider by a fire
Ringing out the old and in the new
Resolutions are quickly forgotten

Warm
Springtime
Sweet flowers
The Earth renewed
So many reasons
To be in a good mood
Some become husbands and wives
We honor mothers and fathers
And remember those who gave their lives
So we can enjoy the freedoms we have

PATIENCE
by Patti Kay Emerson

Patience, they say is a virtue.
But where does it come from?
We're certainly not born with it.
If you don't believe this
Observe a newborn infant.
When a baby wants something,
He wants it now
And screams to get it.
No - Patience must be learned.
And how do we learn it?
It is learned by waiting.
We're always waiting for something:
A doctor's appointment (That's why we're called patients),
A bus, a cab, a child, a parent,
A boyfriend or girlfriend, a student,
A teacher, A grade on a test,
Or a letter in the mail.
This wait is unpleasant at the time
But when it ends we find
It was worth it.
So teach us to wait
And with it bring patience.

THE CHINESE BUFFET
by Gary Reed

When I went for lunch today,
The sign at the Chinese buffet
Redundantly said, "Salmon Fish."

While that may be a fine dish,
I asked for "Salmon Mammal";
Of course, they had none at all.
I gave the server a big smile
And stated, "It's been quite a while,
Since I had some Salmon Reptile."

The reply was curt and hostile.

"Tell the truth," I said, "and don't fib:
Do you have a Salmon Amphibian
Dish, without MSG?"

The cook said emphatically,
"No MSG! You want Cod Fish?"

"Sure," I replied, "It sounds delish."

TRAIN TO NOWHERE
by Patti Kay Emerson

You can set your clock by the train
'Tis always on schedule
At its appointed time.

You know when it's coming
'Cause you feel the vibrations
But never where it comes from
Nor even where it's going,

When it takes you for a ride
Whether or not you want to go
But no matter how long you ride
You always end up back where you started
'Cause it's the train ride to nowhere.

FLYING SOLO
by Liz Shipwash

Off to Grant County High School
For the marching band competition
To see a young girl from Williamstown
With great trumpet ambition.

There will be several school teams
All performing their routines,
It will last many hours
The prize – a trophy with three towers.

The Band of Spirit finally takes the stage
To present "Birds of a Feather"
Karyna's solo at the gilded cage –
Perfect, just like the weather.

Written on September 28, 2013

STORIES

POMP AS A BOY
by Brad Hudepohl

I once asked my grandfather, Pomp, if he had ever done anything mischievous as a boy, and he told me the following story.

At the time Pomp was a boy of twelve, around 1910, it was the style of businessmen in downtown Cincinnati to wear top hats.

In the winter when it snowed, he and a couple of his friends made an arsenal of snowballs. From a distance, and from behind a tall wrought iron fence, they waited for these well-dressed men to pass by on their way home from work. They initiated their attack with the snowballs, trying to knock off their top hats.

Quite often they missed, hitting a gentleman in the ear or face. These men, shouting obscenities and shaking their fists in anger, tried to chase the boys. To avoid repercussions from the infuriated recipients of the attack, Pomp and the other boys quickly ran off, never to be caught.

FRONTIER MESSENGER
Chapter 1: Foundlings
by Alvena Stanfield

Don't rightly know my name. Go by Noah Clark. The foundling home where I growed up was run by Reverend Clark and his wife. They named all of us Clark. Them townfolks knew we wasn't "found." We was tossed out like last night's chamber pot. That's how we was treated, too. Leastwise that's how Joseph explained it to me. He's about four years older than me, smarter and lots bigger. Him and me match up like a long day. He's like night time. All dark with teeth and eyes a person can see with a dirty wick in their lantern. Them teeth sparkle even if I can't make out his face.

Me and Joseph was doing chores.

"You're just like summer at Schroeder's farm," Joseph said. I studied the hens' boxes for a couple minutes while we scrubbed the floor of the coop.

"What are you saying?"

"Look at you. Haystack hair, Summer sky eyes. That's you. Daytime. Me," he said and leaned close, whispering like he was telling me a scary tale like Miz Clark tells. She has a book called Grimm. Scare a kid with terrible dreams all night, leastwise, scares me. Joseph talked real hoarse into my ear.

"Me, I'm like a night with no stars, no moon. I can sneak around and nobody knows. And I can creep up on a body while they's sleeping and…"

Joseph grabbed onto me, drug his index finger across my throat. I about leaped out of the coop, tripped over the dang bucket and landed on the wet floor planks. Them hens went to squawking. I run out hoping the Clarks was busy someplace else. I could hear Joseph laughing along with them chick's squawking as I run toward the summer kitchen.

I could never be mad at Joseph. Reverend Clark made him do men's work. I helped but, skinny me, I never could do what he could. Joseph told me the Reverend called him a beast of burden and threatened to sell him Deep South when he was no taller than Reverend Clark's desk.

"Sell you? That's nothing but crazy talk," I said.

Joseph kicked around at the dust, walked away staring down. I think I saw him wipe his eyes a time or two. I followed him but didn't know what to say.

"We gotta get ourselves to the barn afore the Reverend comes after us," he said. Joseph and me knowed the Reverend liked to use a stick on us. To make sure all of us was watching the Reverend made us sit on long benches watching him. The foundling's eyes would open real wide, squeeze shut, then lips would quiver. He'd sing "We will gather at the river" WHACK. "The beautiful" WHACK. "Beautiful" WHACK. "River" WHACK. All the while he'd be grinning. The Reverend would put striped bruises all over until the foundling begged or wet hisself. So me and Joseph skeedaddled to the barn right quick.

We was getting ready to clean stalls, when me and Joseph heard the steamboat's calliope playing "Beautiful Dreamer." We tossed down our hay forks and took off a-running toward the Cincinnati riverfront. It was near lunchtime and him and me was hoping one of them steamboats was moving out so's we could catch us some vittles. The cooks set them vittles right on Broadway Street's cobblestones.

Never knew what to hope for. Sometimes boiled eggs, sometimes ham, sometimes hot cakes, usually with bites taken out.

Anything, even half eaten hush puppies was better than gruel Miz Clark spooned out for us morning and night. Most times us foundlings was hungry. At the dock a body had to wiggle through a crowd to get to the piles of food. Lots of us Porkopolis folks was hungry. If people didn't grab them quick-like, the pigs or ducks would sure enough gobble them up. Me and Joseph would grab and run or else it'd be jerked away from us. Whatever food fit inside our shirts we hid lessen Reverend Clark took it for himself.

"Back to work you sons of Lucifer," Reverend Clark shouted when he spied us hurrying back from the dock. We run behind a hay wagon so's he wouldn't see our puffed-out shirts. At the barn, we turned a near empty grain bucket upside down where food would hide until we could slip it to the other foundlings. Reverend Clark bragged he was "a breeder of fine horse flesh." Too bad he didn't feed us foundlings as good as the horses.

Like everything else terrible about him, Reverend Clark was a liar. There was six of us what tended them ornery horses. He was no horse breeder. Never saw the Reverend at the barn unless a buyer come by. That's what happened that day in the fall of 1859. That's how we come to meet up with Mister William Waddell of Saint Joseph, Missouri, and I tried on my new and forever name, Pony Noah Clark.

Mr. Waddell tied his horse to the hitch by the barn and ambled toward us.

"I'm William Waddell. The barber told me this is the best horse breeder near Cincinnati. How many horses do you have here to sell?" he said.

He was standing near the paddock where we'd moved the horses while we cleaned stalls. We'd just done putting in new hay and was pumping water (me) and carrying filled buckets (Joseph) to the troths. Horses drank a lot. Anybody eyeing the manure pile in back of the barn knew they ate a lot too.

"I said how many horses are for sale?" he said so loud the palomino run to the other side of the paddock.

Me and Joseph shrugged. We knew to button up our lips. We was afraid we'd say the wrong thing. We'd be at the bad end of Reverend Clark's stick and song. Mr. Waddell shook his head and walked toward the house, then went inside the summer kitchen what was attached. We seen him wiping off his boots so we knowed he was headed into the main house. In the switch of a horse's tail, he was back at the paddock with the Reverend. Me and Joseph headed back to the barn. They come in a few minutes after we let the horses inside.

"These'll all be good mounts for your riders, Sir, but they're worth more than that," Reverend Clark said.

Mr. Waddell opened a stall gate and ran his hand down the nearest horse's shoulder, front leg, then checked the colt's teeth, hooves and chest.

"He's sound as a silver dollar and so are the rest of them," Reverend Clark said.

Mr. Waddell didn't ask me or Joseph, but we would have told him the bay had thrown a shoe and the black mare coughed if she was run hard. But he only talked to the Reverend.

"Okay I'll pay your price. Eight dollars each." The Reverend blinked, no doubt surprised the haggling was over. They shook hands. Mr. Waddell turned and stared at me and Joseph. Joseph stared back at him. I looked down, ashamed like always, and threw another pitchfork of hay into the feeder.

"What about that boy over there?" Mr. Waddell said.

Joseph straightened his back, lifted his chin and grinned.

"Not him, too big, that little skinny one, how old is he? Gotta be thirteen. The California and Pikes Peak Overland Express is hiring," he said as he walked toward us. He handed me a paper.

He handed me a paper

"Can you read, Son?" he said.

"Yes Sir, and me and Joseph can cipher too."

The paper read:

Pony Express
St. Joseph, MO to California in 10 days or less.
WANTED
Young skinny wiry fellows not over eighteen.
Must be expert riders, willing to risk death daily.
Orphans preferred.
Wages $25 per week.
Apply Pony Express Stables St. Joseph Missouri

I stared at the page. $25 a week. Imagine that, a man's wage for just riding a horse.

"Bill Waddell's my name, Son. I'm here looking for riders as well as horses."

My chest swelled up. Nobody'd ever called me "Son" before. For a second I looked him in the eye, then I looked down at my feet all dusty with hay and horse pucks stuck to them.

"Pony Express riders will carry mail from Missouri to California and back. Good wages if a fella can ride a horse like the wind blowing across Indiana," he said.

Didn't know much about riding horses, only how to feed and water them. So, I lied, said I could. Well it wasn't really a lie. I could because I did.

He leaned close to my face. I could smell tobacco.

"What do you say Son?"

I glanced up real quick-like then studied the barn floor.

"Death, Sir? Risk death daily, what's that mean?"

"It means just that. No promises except you get your pay and that's handsome pay."

"Oh yes Sir, but I got no way to St. Joseph stables."

"That's why I booked passage on the Hazel Dell. Captain Metcalf and I have an agreement to move my riders and horses to Hannibal, Missouri. Tomorrow he'll dock at Owensboro. Wherever he stops overnight he gives me time to find riders and horses. I'll be coming back to gather my hired boys before May and drop them off at Hannibal. From there the train will take you to Saint Joseph."

"I got no money, Sir."

Mr. Waddell put his palm on my shoulder.

"I'm paying for passage and food. Each new hire gets a number. Use it on the Hazel Dell and your passage will come out of your first pay."

He rested both his hands on my shoulders.

"Can you ride a horse? Ride it fast all day, all night without a stop?" he said.

"Yes Sir. I sneak to the stable and me and this horse fly like banshees across the…" I lied.

"How old are you? I want fourteen and up."

"I'm thirteen, Sir, nearly fourteen."

The Reverend nodded like he agreed. It was another lie. I was born in 1847 so in fall of '59 I was twelve but since he said he was looking for fourteen I decided I must be. Joseph gave me the evil eye. He knew before I did this was my chance for a new life and he wasn't chosen.

Reverend Clark nodded. "There are more boys in the house," and led Mr. Waddell away.

Later that day Louis, Gabe, Joseph and me stood around Mr. Waddell. He stared at Joseph.

"Make a fist, Boy," he said. He squeezed Joseph's forearm. "You good with horses? Know how to tell a good one from bad?"

"Yes Sir and…." He glanced around real quick to see if the Reverend was nearby, knowing he'd be beat till he peed himself if the Reverend C or his wife heard him. "…and the black mare's shortwinded but she's a good breeder, usually two foals. Last time I had to help her. He was big and stuck, feet first."

"And you knew what to do?" Waddell said.

"Why yes Sir. When she heaved, I pulled. He's out in the paddock. He's already eight hands high."

"Good, I need herd tenders too. The horses come first, understand, before riders."

Joseph straightened real tall, nearly tall as Mr. Waddell.

"I'll be your best herd tender, Sir," Joseph said. Waddell smiled.

"Yes, I believe you. You join these other boys when the Hazel Dell docks for her trip up river." He pulled a small leather book out of his jacket. "Your number is 47." Then he pointed at me. "48." Louis was 49, Gabe 50. Next he read an oath to us. It was a promise to be upright, not to gamble or drink, not to talk bad to or about other riders. One of his business partners would swear us to it in Saint Joseph, Missouri. He unrolled a map.

"Here's stations where the Pony Express stops are circled. About a hundred boys will carry mail two thousand miles," he said.

For $25 a week pay, I sure enough wanted to be a Pony Express rider. The farthest I had ever went was out to old Schroeder's farm with Joseph to pitch hay, had no idea how far a mile was. I soon found out a forty-mile ride was terrible painful.

BURNING REVENGE
by Mikey Chlanda

Heavy black smoke was pouring from all four second-story windows when we rolled up on scene. Jack stopped the rig at the hydrant by the house next door. We were down a guy on our crew, so Jack had to hit the hydrant by himself.

I yelled to Diane and Stevo in the back. "Get ready to rock and roll guys. Stevo, grab the irons...you got entry. Diane, you grab the preconnect. I'll back you."

Picking up the radio mic, I gave my initial size-up. "Osborne 811, Central. This is Osborne Lieutenant 4 establishing Hull Road Command. We have a single occupancy residence two story brick structure, heavy smoke and flame showing on second floor. We're gonna be making initial interior search and attack. Have next arriving officer assume command from me." Not textbook, not what Alan Brunacini taught in the Incident Command Course, but it would have to do. We were short-handed and I would be needed on the interior attack crew more than I was needed as a scene commander.

"Copy," Central came back.

Osborne 806, our ladder truck, came on the air. "Copy direct."

"Hull Road Command, Central. Drop a second alarm. Have units stage behind Osborne 806."

"Copy."

Jack had the hydrant hooked up and was at the pump panel. I leaned across the chauffeur's seat and waved at Jack. The roar of the diesel engine coupled with the noise of the pump engaging made it impossible to be heard. I caught Jack's eye and I motioned to the hydrant. He nodded that he was ready for water. After twenty some-odd years together on the fire department and him being my chauffeur the last twelve, we didn't need to talk to know what the other one meant by a simple hand motion or glance.

I left my seat and opened up the hydrant with the spanner wrench, then got on my portable radio. "Hull Road Command, Osborne 806."

"This is Osborne 806, go Hull Road."

"When you get here, pull in behind me. We'll do primary search...you vent the roof and do secondary. Establish RIT when second due pulls in." RIT was short for Rapid Intervention Team. Two guys, separate hose line from a different engine in case your engine screwed up, ready to go in and haul us out if we got trapped. Those teams had saved a lot of firefighters' lives since the 1990's when they became mandatory.

I yelled to Diane as she was shouldering the hose pack containing four sections, or two hundred feet of preconnect hose. "Belay that order. Get the deuce and a half out with the wye. I'll grab the preconnect and haul it to the door." We weren't going to have enough preconnect to get to the seat of the fire and I wasn't going to chance it. We needed to lay in a deuce and a half and then hook up the preconnect one and three quarter inch line to that. I had to make sure we had enough hose to make the stretch to the seat of the fire. Jack came over our private radio channel. "Safety 1, Lieutenant 4. You're set."

I double-clicked the mic to let him know I got his message. That was the great thing about Jack —water supply was his thing. When he was pumping, I never had to worry about having enough water when I was inside having my ass kicked by the fire.

I uncoupled the preconnect hose from the engine and hoisted the preconnect hose pack over my shoulder. When I got to the house, Stevo was hitting the door hard with the halligan, trying to pry it open. Diane had pulled the deuce and a half and gotten it to the door. She was hooking up the wye when I dropped the preconnect at her side to have her hook it up.

We had just finished connecting it when 806 rolled up. Billy came out of the officer's side and hustled over to me by the front door.

"Hey Jake, I'm here."

I looked up at him. "Billy, you got command." He gave me a thumbs up and went back to the ladder truck. When you pass command, you're supposed to have a face-to-face with the other guy. That had to be one of the fastest pass-offs in history.

"Osborne Lieutenant 6, Central, assuming Hull Road Command. Commencing interior operations."

"Central, Hull Road Command, copy. Osborne Lieutenant 6 assuming Hull Road Command from Osborne Lieutenant 4."

Stevo had the door opened by then. I gave the thumbs up to Jack to charge the line. Stevo cleared the kinks from the deuce and a half as Diane and I finished masking up and turning on our air packs. Diane had the knob. I slapped her on the back and we went in, keeping low.

The heat wasn't bad yet, but it would be once we hit the second floor. The black smoke banked above us making visibility impossible. We kept our right hands on the wall, knowing that typically in these kinds of houses that's where the staircase was.

We went through the mudroom and hit the staircase. The smoke was getting worse. At the top of the staircase we hit the floor, lying prone, trying to escape the 400 degree heat that was just above our heads. I pulled the portable to my mask. "Lieutenant 4, Entry. Open the line."

"Copy." Stevo opened the gated wye and let the water flow into our hose line. Diane and I straightened the line as best we could and starting crawling down the hall. We got to the first door. After checking for backdraft, Diane opened up the nozzle on fog pattern as I kicked open the door.

Black smoke poured out, but no flames. Diane shut down the line and I made a quick search. It seemed like a kid's room, with what seemed to be toys on the floor. It was too small to be a master bedroom. I didn't find anyone as the room was clear. I crawled back out to the door and slapped Diane on the shoulder to let her know.

The heat was getting worse. We made our way to the next door. Our bunkers were already soaked from our sweat on the inside and the water from Diane opening up on fog pattern on the outside of our gear. *Shit, I gotta come up with a better way of losing weight.* It was pretty common to lose eight to ten pounds at a fire scene just from sweat.

"Hull Road Command, Interior."

"Interior, Hull, go." I was breathing too hard from the exertion to answer Billy much more.

"Osborne 806 is now venting roof. RIT in place."

I double-clicked my mic to let him know I got the message. The venting should help clear the smoke and heat, since it would go straight through the gaping hole in the roof, rather than spreading all over the second floor where we were. It would take a few minutes until they finished the job, but it would help.

We made our way down to the next bedroom. Same deal. It, too, was empty. Another kid's room. Stevo came up to join us. I didn't know he was there until he slapped me on the shoulder from behind and scared the shit out of me. I pointed to the room at the end of the hall and leaned over next to the side of his helmet. "Gotta be the bathroom...you search that, I'll take this." I pointed to the room on the left.

Maybe a study or office? There was no bed in there, but what felt like a desk and an office chair, along with some other office furniture, I was guessing. The smoke was getting heavier; visibility was down to about three inches.

We met back up in the hallway two minutes later. Stevo hit me on the shoulder, leaned into me so our masks almost hit each other, and shook his head. He had come up empty too. No victims in either place. Ceiling panels starting coming down on us, one at a time. Nothing to get too excited about, the floors were still solid below us, but it was not a good sign of things to come.

Shit. The way the flames were pouring from the front, but not much interior fire visible so far, this had to be a balloon construction house with no fire stops in the walls. Flames must be shooting from the interior wall of this last bedroom, climbing all over the house between the inside wall and the outside wall, finally venting to the outside on three sides of the house. This house was a goner.

I decided we were pulling out after searching this last bedroom. It was not worth risking my crew's lives anymore after doing the initial search for victims.

I tilted my head to reach the mic hooked to my upper arm and pressed the key. "Interior search, Hull Road Command."

"Hull Road, Interior, go." Billy answered back quickly.

"Most of search done. One bedroom to go. Heavy smoke, heavy heat. Situation becoming untenable. Pulling out shortly."

"Hull Road, Interior. Clear. Your call on pulling out. Venting is done, should be better in a few." Billy knew I wouldn't risk my brothers' lives without a damn good reason.

Beams started falling on us as we regrouped and headed for the master bedroom. Diane opened the line on fog again and Stevo pushed the door all the open. Flames shot out above our heads. We all went prone on the floor and belly crawled. The temperature felt like it rose another 200 degrees.

We couldn't hear anything except for our breathing. Diane in the lead had the line open all the way, dumping 250 gallons a minute on the fire, making headway. Stevo and I headed opposite ways to cut the search time in half. He would do left search, keeping his left hand on the wall, and I would do right search, keeping my right hand on the wall. We would meet in the middle, knowing we had covered the whole room.

As I was doing the right hand search, sweeping my halligan with my left hand around the room as I made my way around, my left leg hit something soft. I felt around more and it was definitely a victim. I gave a tug on the body. Light, maybe a teenager?

I got on the radio. "Lieutenant 4, Command, got a vic. Ladder C side rear window." On any fire scene, our department labelled the front wall facing the first due engine the "A" side. The left side as you faced the building was the "B" side, the right side was the "C" side, and the rear was "D" side. This way there was no confusion as to which side you were talking about.

"Copy. Ladder C side rear window."

Diane had the fire pretty well knocked down by then, helping with the heat level. 806's venting had done a good job starting to clear the smoke and the remaining heat. Diane backed off the hose a little, not pouring quite as much water, hitting the numerous hot spots still remaining.

I started dragging the victim over to the side window. When I got there, I rose up to my knees on one side of the window. I used the halligan to knock the panes of glass out, then ran it around the frame to knock out any shards that were still there.

Billy's crew already had the ladder in place and one of them was coming up. I brushed off the window sill one more time and lifted the victim up make the handoff. We made the exchange when I felt Stevo behind me. He had another victim. He pointed in the direction he had come from and held up two fingers. *Shit. Two more victims?*

Visibility was starting to clear –it was maybe two or three feet now, with the heat much better. I headed off in the direction Stevo had pointed. He hoisted his victim over the sill and waited for another firefighter to come up the ladder.

I found another victim on the master bed –an adult female from the looks of it. I got up to my knees and putting my arms under her underarms, dragged her over to the window. I handed her off to Stevo and he hoisted her over the window sill, waiting for the next firefighter to come up the ladder.

He grunted as his low-air alarm went off. He started hitting it, trying to shut it off, wiggling his air pack, trying to get some more time. We always called him "Heavy Breather" or "Pervert", since he seemed to always drain his air pack first. The rest of our air packs would be emptying soon. We had less than five minutes to get the last victim out and get out ourselves before we ran out of air.

I went back for the last victim. Diane had the fire pretty well knocked down by now. The heat was bearable and the visibility was up to about five or six feet on the floor, maybe three or four feet when kneeling.

I went to the other side of the bed, breathing hard, standing up now in the relatively clear room. Lying on his stomach, it looked like an adult male. As I bent over to grab the guy by his underarms, I rolled him over to get a better grip.

Holy shit. His face looked like it had been blown away by a shotgun.

What the hell did we get ourselves into here?

MY COMMENCEMENT:
A Memoir
by Elle Mott

College is a time to prepare for new beginnings into a career life. New beginnings, however, can come in a multitude of ways and not exclusive to one's career. On my commencement day, I couldn't imagine a fulfilling future, but instead wallowed in denial that my life was forever changed. Little did I know then, my strength as gained from my campus friends and peers had prepared me for life after college; a life of happiness, purpose, and meaning.

My classmates had spent spring semester job interviewing for their new life whereas I had barely touched a job application. Instead, spring semester for me had been one of complacency because I couldn't face the fact that my world as I knew it had to end. I was not ready for commencement because I couldn't fathom life anywhere else, but I didn't dare show my sadness. My peers looked up to me and always had, whether it was when in my role as club president, as student advocate, as a library page, or as a mentor, friend, or ally. I couldn't let them down. Never had before, and wouldn't on our final day together.

I wanted to crawl back into my world of denial rather than be there in that green graduation gown, feeling strangled by the yellow honor sash as it crossed my body. Well dressed, if only to rise above the standards of my own style, all which showed from under my graduation garb was my paisley necktie, tightly knotted where revealed by the v-neckline. Paisley may have gone out of style years before, but I liked the individuality and nonconformity it suggested, even though my choice might have dated me as I waited with classmates half my age for the procession.

The year prior I could have passed as just a little older than them but on that day, the youth in my face was gone, weathered by the sweat and tears I had poured into my campus life for three years. Nor was I a scrawny teenager, but buff with a buzz haircut as if to make a political statement on my five-foot-one stature. Other than my necktie, my black patent oxfords showed. They were polished, should someone have bothered to look down.

If it weren't for the cap and gown I wore, same as the other students, I could easily have been mistaken for a teacher in Fine Arts or maybe even Phys. Ed. Certainly not a professor, because they were easy to spot with their greyed hair, wrinkles and reading glasses that either dangled lopsided off their nose or else on a chain at their full bosom. Many glances from afar made their way to me then stopped for a smile before looking elsewhere. In reality, though, I likely received no more looks than anyone else.

There I stood on that day of commencement in one of many clusters of classmates, gathered together in the outdoor alcove to the gymnasium. I remembered my first day on campus, just days after I had arrived in Seattle. Classes weren't even in session then when I saw a young woman tack flyers on a bulletin board. Giant evergreen trees served as the canopy on the paved pathways. The sun was warm but with a not so gentle breeze. I had caught up to her and reached out my hand to help. I held the flyer flat as she pushed the thumbtack in.

A year after the day I helped her post flyers, it was me who posted them. It was invitational flyers to our club, first known as the Rainbow Club. Yet at the end of my first year in as a student, I was club co-president, and we had changed our club name to Project Pride. I had helped make real change on campus in that we set labels aside and rallied for an all-inclusive learning environment by advocating for diversity by challenging school policies. We were the most outspoken club on campus, and through it I shared camaraderie with others.

Six days a week on campus was the norm for me. In the early mornings and all day on Sundays, I had my job in the campus library. Lunches were with club friends. Afternoons were study time with classmates. The hours in between meant time to advocate for student rights, mentor a peer, participate in a charity drive, or to let loose and have fun at a campus event.

Breaks in between semesters were no exception to the rule. Winter breaks found me in holiday parties or another charity drive with Phi Theta Kappa, the International Honor Society. Summer breaks put me with my club members as we moved our activism to the greater community, to march in the Seattle Pride Parade, for one. The summer break just before year two was spent in leadership retreats and preparation for the new school year as one of twelve members elected into Student Government.

As student advocate, I found myself in the middle of change for our campus. It was the year our college's student government went from a bicameral body with executive and legislative branches to a parliament. We were a new way of doing things and as such, we operated as one team and not two as before known. We each had our own job, under the leadership of one faculty member, and always accountable to the School Board. Our offices were in a brand new building, the Student Leadership Center. But, on Friday afternoons, which often stretched into three or four hours, we came together for our open business meeting in the Administrative Building.

I had certain hours on the paid clock, but one wouldn't know it because I refused to limit myself to such constraints. I didn't see it as an intrusion when someone came to me, even though I could have been head deep into my own studies. Students had an array of problems, from grades to teachers to bullying, and I was the up-front liaison to resolve any unfriendly messes.

During my year on Student Government, I occasionally volunteered as a mentor in the International Student Program. Then, in my last year, I filled up hours to give more one-on-one time to students who were brand new, not only to our campus, but to our country. Likened to my club activism for an all-inclusive campus community, I learned from those I mentored. They taught me their foreign customs and values, and enlarged my friendship circle.

My memories were interrupted as a classmate jumped out of her group and into mine. She gave me a big hug and said, "Congratulations, we did it."

Yes, *"did,"* as in past tense, was so true in my mind's eye. I saw the gymnasium door ahead swing open and everyone fell back into their respective clusters as the procession into the auditorium began. I stepped in line and followed the gal in front of me.

I took my seat and looked to the sidelines. Krista whistled kisses to me. I knew many of my classmates had moms and dads in the audience. I had Krista. And two other gal friends. They had more beaming pride for me than anyone could ever ask for. Three years prior I had arrived in Seattle, not knowing anyone, except for my professor who I had known only from my application and admission process. That's when I met my friend Krista and while she grew her business, I grew in my own ways, in my campus life.

Mr. Backes spoke into the microphone and welcomed everyone. He was the campus Vice President of Academic Affairs, the overseer of all deans, and a familiar face to me. We had talked countless times, sometimes with all seriousness in my student advocate role. Just as often, though, we had talked over nothing more than the rainy weather or the recent presidential campaign between Obama and McCain.

My attention drifted from his monotone voice that only heightened my dismal awareness toward my future. I thought to myself, "It's a good thing teachers can't poke at my brain now. They'd discover me deep in thought far from the moment in time." What I really wanted to say out loud if I could was, "Poof, whoosh, vamoose, no more; it's done and gone, forevermore."

Perhaps if I had been at a normal college age, the transition would have been easier. But as it was, I was in my early forties, significantly older than those I had melded with for three years. I should have looked forward to a career job, but I no longer desired my degree choice and I had no job lined up. I couldn't even keep my campus library job because being a student was a requirement. In fact, I'd lose many privileges as I passed over from being a student to being an outsider.

I wish I could say all fell well into place after that day. To the contrary, I did not know where to go or what to do when two days later, on Monday, the emptiness inside me was weighted with an intense ache for the life that was no longer mine to be had. As a child, Nana had instilled in me to have a purpose in everything I did and to go after anything I wanted. I ran with that idea in college. I couldn't leave college only to falter in those expectations. I had to move forward and make my late nana proud of me for being a strong young woman, not far from fifty years old.

I was in the awakening fall-out of the 2008-09 recession and unemployed. America's economic downfall only hurt any opportunities for potential employers to take a chance on me. I was not going to be given a new life. I did not have a mommy or daddy to go home to, and I didn't have a spouse or kids I was accountable to. It was up to me to want a new life and then to make that new life. In my search for personal revival, I drifted in valleys from coast to coast until I landed in Northern Kentucky, my place to finally call home.

When in those valleys, the only thing that lifted my spirits was to remember I had potential. To give credit to those who had once believed in me pushed me to find my place. Even when I went broke, I found fortitude. I lost my career path as studied for in college because I couldn't financially keep up on my professional credentials, but in turn fell back on my love for the working world inside libraries.

Like I had been active with the Project Pride Club, today I am an active member with a regional group that seeks to make positive change in social justice issues. Where Phi Theta Kappa had shown me to care about others, today I show up to toil in shared volunteer commitments. My peers in the International Student Program had given me an appreciation for different cultures, and today I like to celebrate with others, even if their way is a new idea to me.

Where I had once thrived in my campus community, today I thrive in being a part of my neighborhood community with fervor for developing personal strengths and valuing the strengths in others. The Covington Writers Group is one place I'm easily able to enjoy these opportunities. Likened to when in college, I have discovered many friendly people and appreciate being welcomed into their world, where together we come together as one to develop friendships and better our community.

Today my life is different, built upon more than three years in my new time and place, and with new people, here in Northern Kentucky and the greater Cincinnati area. But the real difference comes from the power instilled by the values I gained not only from Nana, but from my campus peers. I had been given opportunities in college to make a real difference with positive outcomes; outcomes that I did not see on that day in my green graduation gown and paisley tie, struggling to commence. Today my life is happy, with purpose and meaning, along with gratitude for those who have walked with me, whether then or now.

MAYHEM WITH A BEER CHASER
by L. N. Passmore

Some considered Fritz odd. He gave up a steady job the day he got sunstroke in the Kentucky oil fields. Although he had worked oil all over the Appalachians, the stroke set off a wanderlust that took him "out of the rigs and into the woods," he said, "collecting specimens and mysteries."

Maybe that's what turned him into a spinner of tall tales.

"Lies!" according to his proper German sisters.

He finally landed in Lexington to live with these ladies, who disapproved of drinking beer.

"Devil's brew" they called it.

One sweltering summer day while hiding out in the grape arbors with Eber and Rein, a couple of his cronies, he pulled a red bandana from his overalls. His brow and neck swabbed, he declared, "Lordy, it's hot enough to roast chickens in the coop."

Tipping back his chair against one of the arbor palings, he cautioned, "Keep a lookout for my sisters, a bunch of worrisome *hausfrau*, always reforming the life out of a man, but they beat me at cooking." Fritz winked, "except for my fried squirrel."

He shook his head and downed a beer. The belch he let out made his potbelly bounce.

***

After his buddies' laughter choked down to a pleased hiss, he recalled a yarn:

I mind a worrisome hot day, back in my time of black gold and amber beer at Humity Dulin's General Store. What Missus Dulin called a Food and Dry Goods *Emporium.*

Humity set up trade in Beattyville where the three forks of the Kentucky River come together. It's the Lee County Seat, don't you know, not far from the Big Sinking, a right smart oil field. I was working the oil rigs back then.

His place was so dark that we oil riggers threatened to wear miner's hats. Humity snorted. "Light ain't free."

We riggers came in for beer river-shipped from Louisville, tobacco, glazed crullers, and any news from beyond Big Sinking. Knowing we'd swap tales of the latest doings at the rigs, Humity grinned and waved.

***

Fritz laughed and looked over at Eber and Rein to make certain they were paying attention and then over his shoulder in case one of his sisters had tracked him to his hideout. Satisfied, he continued:

Well now, I headed straight for the pickle tub, and John Vogler tried to wheedle a beer on the house. Humity kept a tap behind the meat counter.

You betcha Humity balked at that. "Buy something to go with that briner, Fritz," he bellowed, "and tell your friend that he'll not be lollygagging here for free." He picked up a fly swatter and crushed a big one that had settled on the meat scales.

On about the hottest day an August had ever seen, Humity was having one of his "mad-ons," as Missus Dulin called his fits. Fly strips hanging from the ceiling looked like bark. The coolest spot in the store was the January igloo on the Miss Co'-Cola calendar.

"Hey, Humity, don't you know it's August?" Vogler called out as the sweat dropped from his mustache on to the oiled oak floor. 'When you going to change the calendar?"

Humity scowled. "When you pay your bill!"

Heat lightning prickled my backbone; should have known Humity had a head of steam building. Well, we plopped ourselves in front of the big window facing East Main. I put my back to the glass. After a spell on the rigs, my favorite sport was just leaning back and watching it all unroll at Dulin's. I watched him hammer-fist some chopped meat, part red, part brown, up to the scale. A lady, a cut above most, dressed right smart, all clean and starched, leastways her flowered dress didn't look like a crumpled sheet, attempted to keep two *kinder* from squirming and pinching each other.

Vogler nudged me. "The Leering Woman."

***

Fritz threw up his hands and stamped his feet.

Lordy, oh Lordy, Missus Leering, come with Clarence and Lillie—the Imps of Beattyville, better known as Devil and Deep Blue.

Clarence had tar black hair, brows thick as my thumb, sallow skin, and yellow rattlesnake eyes. He lowered the temperature considerable for all he was just seven years old. His sister, maybe a year older, made me wonder if one was adopted. Clarence's hair shone like a summer pump handle, but Lillie had heaps of knotted russet ringlets. With big black-fringed eyes under that tawny mane she looked like a raccoon. No matter, they were two peas in a pod for orneriness.

As I say, my back neglected the finer sights of a mostly muddy East Main. The night before, the sky had opened up to drench Beattyville. I commenced to survey the possibilities for the rapscallions to enhance their reputation. You should know that Humity had recently installed a flush-toilet indoor privy—all by himself, no proper plumber—and mighty proud of it he was. Humity's Missus considered it private but accommodated emergencies. That poor woman.

Now, Missus Leering went to survey the dry goods, Lillie trailing after her. That's when Clarence waylaid his mother, his hand playing nervously before his crotch. In my experience, any mother worth her salt pounces on the slightest hint of . . . you know, misuse of *parts*. Missus Leering startled Humity with a baffling announcement: "Mr. Dulin, my Clarence is now of an age at which he needs no help in completing his functions!"

***

Fritz waggled his white eyebrows.

She arched one brow and tilted her head, pointing to the new oak door where the pantry next to the Dulin kitchen used to be. Humity stood there, leaning on the pickle tub, no wiser. His Missus rounded the corner of the vegetable bins and tin canned goods, glanced at the stalled figures—Clarence's hand inching to dangerous territory, his knees beginning to buckle—and dragged the child to the privy.

Lillie seized her chance. "Mother, where is my toy?"

Missus Leering raised her other eyebrow. Missus Dulin, Esther or Hester I think her given name was, pointed the child in the opposite direction, towards John and me and the bins with the gee-jaws. Lillie cut a straight path to the china elephants and squirt guns, touched a few, sizing them up, and then sashayed up to us.

"I'm Lillie Leering." She stood before us with her sunburned arms crisscrossed over her chest.

"Yes, my dear," said I. "What shall we do about that?"

She smirked. "Oh, you don't have to do a lick. Clarence and I will manage quite nicely. You work for the Oil Company, don't you?"

"How do you know that, Miss Lillie?"

"I know all about everything; it's my job, and a much nicer one than Mother's, but then, she has to mind us and the new baby, which I hope Aunt Tillie has lost by the time we get home."

You can see how she was. With my change as legal tender, Vogler headed to the tap for yet another beer. I surveyed the compound. The Regulator clock off to my left over the cash register let out a dull "thung." Its brass pendulum swung back and forth, left . . . right . . . left.

Vogler and Humity commenced to argue about what *really* happened the night our proprietor took a plunge into Grogan's Marsh off the South Fork of the river. I've got to tell you. . . .

***

He paused, winked, then squinched his eyes, drawing Eber and Rein into a deep secret. It was only a usual fishing mishap, not planned, not something a man wants to explain, especially as it got George Dulin christened with a name guaranteed to recall his tumble, slap-down, with the beer keg right on top of him.

Humity went fishing for the beer. Now there's a man who hated getting wet, not to mention how he loathed any weather with *humidity* higher than an Arizona desert. It put him right in a rage.

"Blast this humity!" he'd growl. "Dadgummy muggy humity make my skin crawl."

As long as I'd known George, just as soon as March tumbled into April he'd commence to curse the "humity."

When we saw George crawl from the oil-slickered bog that used to be an ordinary marsh, Big Red bawled out, "Now that's Humity!" It stuck. But then so did the black gunk, all over Humity's . . . hmm . . . let's say *hefty* soaked body. When he got up a good head of hate, he swelled to about the size of a steam boiler on the old Chessie train. Humity didn't trifle when it came to venting a whole barrelful of wrath.

***

He closed his eyes and smiled.

"Fritz," Eber said, setting down his third bottle, "What about the Devil and Deep Blue?"

48

Fritz chuckled.

Ja . . . my other story! So . . . I saw Lillie mosey around each bin, touching every corner, all the while eying the privy. My scalp tingled. Deep Blue turned her head, cat like, watching a hole for a fat mouse. Her gaze widened, took in that whole store, all the bins, racks, and counters, flypaper too.

Soon enough, Clarence exited the little john stall, having discharged his functions, no doubt, when Lillie joined him for some kind of boss-talk palaver. Devil looked my way, then to the privy, back to Deep Blue, and finally bent his head down to the floor, but that didn't hide his grin. They chortled, their heads stuck together, just like two weasels asked to guard the hen house.

Hell's bells! In came three ladies, all carrying shopping baskets and holding lists that could outfit the next three Christmases. Humity's answering five questions at once, weighing out some sausage, and keeping an eye on the coffee pot perking on the gas stove. He made no truce with August. "Sweat is sweat," he'd say. "Being soaked in this gawd-awful muggy weather is no reason to give up my coffee."

Of course, I kept track of Devil and Deep Blue. I swear they conjured up the dark angel fixing to blow the lid on mischief and mayhem. Smiling as sweet as an orphan at review time down at the home, Lillie picked up a china elephant. She walked to the privy.

Clarence examined a red water gun, pushing in its plunger and judging its range. He slid along the left wall, by the counter with the cash register, and advanced on the privy. Hissing clouds of dark-spicy coffee aroma erupted just as one of the ladies pinned Humity against the meat counter. She was screeching about green pork chops. And then . . . Devil and Deep Blue went into the privy. Together!

***

Rein blurted, "What?" and Eber followed, "With their mother, God, and everyone right there?"

Fritz's head bobbed up and down.

First out was Clarence, wiping his hands on his pants. I looked for Missus Leering among the stacks of dry goods. She and Humity's Missus unrolled a bolt of crab apple pink cloth and draped it over Missus Leering's shoulder. Clarence hid the water gun behind his back as he faced Humity, directly up the aisle from Vogler and me. I nudged Vogler to turn around. "Put down that beer. Here comes a good one, by God!" I said.

The old Regulator didn't lose a beat.

Out of the privy came Lillie. Empty-handed!

By now, Vogler's several beers had worked their way through his considerable plumbing, and attention being drawn to the indoor privy, he decided to use the facilities, he, too, being capable of completing his functions. The rebel angel hovered, casting a red haze on the heat of that August day.

Just like all of us raised to leave the barn door open, Vogler forgot to latch the door. The flush—whooping and coughing and whooshing up from the ground, and around that porcelain bowl—made a racket fit to wake the dead. But the sight of Vogler, his pants soaked and dragging, popped all our eyes. Vogler set off a deluge.

Lillie had plugged the toilet with that china elephant, and somehow all the innards of that water pumping marvel crammed together then blew. The water flowed fit to raise the Ark.

Humity let out a yowl. The women wailed and covered their eyes. They ran like Sunday chickens. Vogler took a sharp veer to his right and tangled in the bolt of pink cloth. Clarence took aim. He squirted old Humity on his red face with that water pistol, filled—you guessed it—with water from that very same commode.

That stopped Humity dead, the pressure gauge at about a thousand pounds per square inch! The drill head burst all over that store. Fly paper shook to the timbers. Every, I mean every, button on Humity's shirt popped, arcing up and out, plop, plop, hitting pickles and onions, and Missus Tilson right in the eye. By then we were ankle deep in the flow from the privy.

Humity crashed through the door and wrenched that white contraption, root and all, from the floor, which only added to the fountain. Humity's own Yellowstone natural wonder!

What could he do? He sat on that gushing pipe and groaned something pitiful to anyone to shut off the water.

His Missus bawled, "George! I told you not to put that thing in yourself!"

Vogler, his pants now buckled, leaped at the opportunity, dragging me with him, and called, "Oh Humity, you butt cork you, this calls for another beer!"

THE BRIDGE
by Jenny Breeden

Author Note: The 1892 Licking River bridge collapse was a historical event, and some of the names and details used in this story are factual, researched in *Kentucky Enquirer* newspaper articles and old Covington City Directories by the author The restaurant, the main characters, and their conversations are fictional, based solely on the imagination of the author. *J.B.*

Monday, June 13, 1892

Every morning usually started the same, with chores and deliveries, but today was different. After Harold installed the fresh ice blocks into the upper compartments of the two huge wooden ice boxes, Millie walked with him out to his wagon. She wanted to be at the curb when the Hatterman's Dairy wagon rolled up. On any other morning, she would be inside doing chores when she'd hear the hooves clattering on the cobblestones. Some days, she'd barely make it out in time to say "good morning" to the driver as he finished unloading her milk, butter, eggs and cheese. Other times, she'd have a few extra minutes to chat with him about his family, the weather or the like. This morning, she had something important to ask him and didn't want to miss the opportunity.

"How is Paul doing?" Mille asked the driver as soon as he pulled up. "Any change yet?"

"Afraid not, Miss Millie," the young man said, stepping down from the wagon seat. "Still unconscious…same as when they found him last Thursday morning…laying in the middle of the street."

"I'm so sorry to hear that, Michael. I've been worried sick about him and his poor family. I read in the *Enquirer* that they think he was driving too fast. Say he tried to make the turn onto Pike Street and was thrown from his seat."

"I heard the same thing from Old Man Hatterman," Michael replied. "Doc Murnan over at the hospital don't hold out much hope for Paul's recovery." He put the milk bottles and other items on the ground near Millie. "Says if he ain't come around by now, he probably ain't gonna."

"Oh, my. That's just awful," Millie said solemnly. "I'll keep saying prayers for him." As the driver climbed back into the wagon, she added, "Michael, you be careful on those turns yourself. Can't have anything happen to you, now can we?"

"No, Ma'am, we can't." He smiled, knowing that she was sincere in her concern for his welfare. "See ya tomorrow, Miss Millie." He drove off to make his next delivery.

As she finished putting the last of the dairy into the smaller of the two ice boxes, Millie saw her workers coming in the back door; their hand carts piled high with sacks of fruits and bushels of vegetables from Fieger's market.

When they had stowed away most of the items, Millie passed out assignments. "Connie, you snap the green beans today, and Sally, you peel potatoes. I'll make the biscuit dough." Both young ladies nodded and started to work without saying a word.

By the time they finished their tasks, the sun was peeking over the trees that lined the riverbank. They had several pots simmering on the stoves, several trays of biscuits baking in the ovens and about five minutes to relax before the place opened to greet the first batch of customers for breakfast.

Sally and Connie were chatting at one of the tables near the front entrance. Millie poured herself a half cup of coffee and sat at one of the tables near the kitchen. Picking up the Monday morning edition of the *Enquirer*, she skimmed the headlines.

"I can't wait 'til the election's over," she said aloud but to no one in particular. "We still got four months until Election Day, and that's all those reporters can talk about." She took a sip, scowling at a headline announcing Harrison was nominated on the first ballot at the National Convention in Minneapolis. "Who cares anyhow? None of us can even vote."

With that comment, Connie chimed in. "My Alex says that's a good thing…seeing as how we women don't know the first thing about politics. Besides, he says I needn't worry my pretty head about such things."

Sally giggled. "Daddy's votin' for Harrison again. Cleveland had his chance to be re-elected in '88, and he missed it. He's all washed up as a politician." She was obviously parroting her father's words. She stood up and walked over to unlock the front door. "Whitmore's Restaurant is officially open for the day's business," she announced cheerfully.

That signaled the end of their too short break. From five thirty on, they had a steady stream of men coming in, most for the daily special —two scrambled eggs, fried bacon, a buttermilk biscuit and coffee for two bits. Others just wanted coffee and a quick glance at the newspaper.

"Aw, them lousy Reds…lost again to the Boston Beaneaters." The man slammed the sports page on the table in disgust.

To that, his friend replied, "Dem bums ain't got a prayer this year." They both laughed and finished their coffee, each leaving a nickel on the table.

Millie unfortunately had to agree with their opinion, but she didn't offer any comment. Even though she tried to keep up with the local happenings, she learned not to butt into conversations unless they specifically engaged her. However, if someone wanted to strike up a conversation, she was more than ready.

It was also important to know the goings on in case she had newcomers visit her place. If they asked, "What is there to do in this town?" she wanted to be ready to offer up several suggestions, depending on the time of year. In the summer, they had baseball over in Cincinnati and horse racing at the Latonia Jockey Club. Millie's favorite places to visit were the Cincinnati Zoo, Music Hall and the Art Museum. Of course, they weren't everyone's cup of tea.

Seeing that Connie and Sally were busy collecting money from the tables their customers had just left, Millie grabbed the coffee pot from the stove and headed to the only occupied table. She filled up the cups for the two men sitting there. Everyone else had already cleared out a few minutes before the seven a.m. whistle blew, signaling the start of the morning shift at the mill. These men however, dressed in suits instead of overalls, were not in any hurry. They continued to talk while they finished their breakfast. Millie began clearing dirty dishes from the nearby tables.

"I'm telling you the false work around the bridge isn't strong enough to hold the weight of the traveler and the iron girders."

"You worry too much, Frank. My brother and I have designed many bridges."

"I AM worried. You weren't up there when the whole thing shook…"

"You're talking nonsense." Pointing his right index finger at him, he continued, "Listen to me. The Memphis Bridge used the same wooden support structure and it worked just fine.

His tone wasn't very reassuring, Millie thought. In fact, it sounded rather condescending.

"But I'm the one in charge of building *THIS* bridge… and, uh… I don't think it's fine at all." He pounded the table. "It's my reputation on the line. Hell, it's *MY* crew at risk."

The other man smiled. "If it's any comfort, I've wired Andrew. He's coming out from our Pittsburgh office to do a full inspection."

"Good. I hope I can talk some sense into him." Frank lowered his voice a bit. "When does he arrive?" Although he sounded calmer, his furrowed brow gave Millie an uneasy feeling.

"On the Fifteenth, Wednesday morning. He's coming straight to the construction site from the train station."

After he sipped the last of his coffee, Frank swallowed hard. "Guess I can wait two more days."

The men didn't seem concerned about the level of their voices or that someone might overhear their conversation. In fact, Millie figured they were either oblivious to her presence, or they thought she was too stupid to understand what they were talking about. Maybe they thought she didn't know who they were. She watched as each man rose from his chair, left a quarter on the table, and headed out into the street.

As she cleared the dishes from their table, Millie replayed their conversation in her head. She did know who the two men were, and they were talking about the Licking River Bridge. The whole thing made her extremely nervous. Frank was Frank Muir, the foreman in charge of the bridge construction project. The other man in the conversation was Robert Baird, one of two brothers who were contracted to design the bridge. That bridge was important to a lot of people, but for Millie, it was the reason she was here —running a restaurant all by herself. Her thoughts drifted back to another fateful conservation over breakfast she'd had with her husband, George, when he had first heard talk of a new bridge.

"I have a great idea," George had announced that morning with an excitement Millie had rarely seen since they had laid their only son, William, into his grave some four years earlier. "You know that old abandoned house on Twelfth Street, near the river?" He could tell from her confused look she didn't know what house he was talking about. "Between Greenup and Garrard? You know, the one I said looks like it might fall down in a strong storm?"

Millie had nodded her head, acknowledging she knew it.

"Well, I noticed yesterday they've hung a for sale sign on the front door."

"So what?" Millie wondered where he was going with this.

"It's less than one square from where they're talking about putting in a new bridge across the Licking. Barely three squares down from the Rolling Mill." He took a bite of his eggs and swallowed fast. "I think we can get it cheap...do some remodeling. Of course, I'd have to apply for a permit to do business there but...I'm thinking it's big enough to convert into a restaurant." He paused to observe his wife's expression. She wasn't frowning, so he continued.

"We can fix the upstairs into a small apartment for the two of us, sell this house and get away from the bad memories." He took another bite of eggs. "It'll be a lot of hard work getting it ready. But once we're open, we'll have plenty of business."

"I don't know..."

"And the best part... I'll be my own boss. No more taking orders from a man who has no clue what it takes to run a business."

Millie thought that George apparently had been thinking about his restaurant idea for a while. The "For Sale" sign going up was a 'sign' telling him to get moving on it or lose out to someone else. He had even given some thought to the amount of business a restaurant in that area could draw, since there wasn't one in the mainly residential area. The Licking Rolling Mill employed more than fifty men across the three shifts. If they went through with the talk and built a bridge, the year-long construction would supply many more workers and visitors. Once the bridge opened, the traffic on Twelfth Street would increase and so would the numbers of folks wanting a good meal.

"If that's what you want to do...then I'm behind you one hundred percent," Millie said, thinking she would most likely end up as the cook, waitress and dishwasher while

George handled the day-to-day business, such as hiring staff, keeping the books, and conversing with the patrons as they ate.

"Great! I'll call the number on the sign…see how much they're asking for the place. Can't be too much, considering its condition. I'm sure there'll be a lot of paperwork involved." George was beaming when he kissed Millie good-bye and left for work.

That fateful conversation was only a year ago, but it seemed like a lifetime; so much had happened since then.

"George was right, this place is in the perfect location," Millie whispered to herself. "Too bad he isn't around to enjoy the benefits of all his hard work to get this place up and running."

Brushing away a tear from her eye, she went looking for her help. She found them in the kitchen. Connie was washing dishes, and Sally was drying them as fast as she could to keep up. They needed all of them and more to handle the lunch crowd. Mondays were the busiest day of the work week. The fact that she served her now famous pan-fried chicken, mashed potatoes, green beans and cornbread biscuits probably helped draw in the crowds. Millie watched the two women work in tandem for a few minutes, wondering how they managed to get along so well, especially since they were complete opposites.

Connie Thomas was about twenty, married and trying to start a family. She was only working temporarily to earn some extra money. She'd informed George and Millie five months ago when he hired her that she would be quitting as soon as she got pregnant and was far enough along "to be too big to work." Then, of course, she'd be at home until the baby was born. She said they were planning to have a house full of young'uns. The problem was, she and Alex, her husband, had been trying to get pregnant for a couple of years without any luck.

For her own sake, Millie hoped that it would still be a while before Connie made any happy announcements. She didn't want to have to replace her any time soon. Although she figured she would have to once the bridge was finished and Alex had to find other work. Millie saw how he watched her as she was working. He watched the men too, making sure they weren't eying his woman. She was sure Alex wouldn't let Connie continue to work in the restaurant if he couldn't stop in everyday to check on her.

By contrast, Sally Jenkins turned thirteen last month. The fourth oldest of ten, six boys and four girls, she'd already vowed never to marry. Even if she did marry someday, she said she was most definitely not having any children. On occasion, she'd even threatened her parents with joining a convent. "My only way of gettin' some peace and quiet," she'd said. She had at least one more year of school, maybe more if her parents let her go to high school.

Out for the summer, her father told her, "Go out and make yourself useful." Working at Whitmore's would help her learn to cook and be self-sufficient. At least that's what she told Millie two weeks ago when she waltzed in and asked for a job. How could Millie resist? Sally's youthful enthusiasm was refreshing, so she hired her on the spot.

They'd had a steady run of patrons from about eleven o'clock. Most of them were regulars, coming in for the Monday special. It was nearly noon when a group of eight men came in. Millie had not seen any of them before, but she'd heard that they'd added a bunch of new bridge workers over the past few weeks. With the piers on each end finished, they needed more men to work on installing the span across the river. The group seated themselves at a long table in the tent section.

The tent was a temporary structure installed at the side of the restaurant which extended into the yard. Accessible from the street or through the doorway that connected it to the building part of the restaurant, it doubled the seating capacity. It also increased the profitability of the place from mid-May through late September, until it started getting too chilly to eat outdoors.

The men were discussing something when Millie walked up to greet them. One man seemed extremely agitated.

"By gawd, the whole damn thing's gonna come down…you mark my words!"

"Aw, hush up now, Murray," a younger man, practically a teenager, said to him. "That ain't no way to talk 'round a lady." He looked up to address Millie. "You gotta scuze him, Ma'am…workin' 'round men all morning, and he done forgot all his manners." He laughed.

"Damn it, Dick!" Murray shouted, waving his fist at him. "Don't you be shushin' me. I gotta right to say my mind." His face was red hot.

Another man, just a few years older than the first but with similar facial features, jumped up. "Don't be starting no trouble, Reardon…'specially not with my little brother or I'll…"

To stop them from coming to blows, Millie quickly intervened. "Good afternoon, Gentlemen. Y'all want today's fried chicken special or something from the menu?" She noticed several of the men had their empty beer pails with them. "If y'all want beer, Charlie's at your service."

Most of the men smiled and nodded.

She called for Charlie, Sally's scrawny fourteen-year-old brother. He was spending his summer rushing the growlers from Whitmore's to Sweeney's during lunch time. Each one cost a nickel to fill at the tavern. He called them "growlers" because, when his father or grandfather sent him to fetch a pail of fresh beer, if he wasn't careful and spilled some on the way, the old man would growl at him.

Charlie learned at an early age to be careful not to slosh any beer. For every rush he made, he earned a few pennies, maybe even a nickel. Millie gave him a free meal as her part of their working arrangement. As he collected the nickels and the pails from the men who wanted beer, Millie took their food orders.

In no time, Charlie was back with the six full pails. He carried them using a long notched pole balanced across his shoulders with three pails on each side. He put them on the table without spilling a drop. Each man grabbed the one bearing his mark. Millie noticed a few extra coins changing hands, and she smiled at Charlie; her way of saying "good job"

As she placed the food and the bill slip in front of each man, she overheard snippets of their conversation. It was the man named Murray Reardon who was still doing most of the talking.

"The false work got done Friday. Come Saturday morning, they rolled out the first girder…the whole thing shook like a leaf in the breeze."

"But the foreman wouldn't have us working out there if…"

"Jack, you don't know nuthin'," Murray interrupted. "You and your brothers ain't never built a bridge before. I have. But I ain't never seen the likes of this."

"Maybe the foreman don't know how bad it is," Dick said.

"Oh, he damn sure knows it…I told Frank Muir weeks ago and again Saturday morning," Murray said. "He's a Democrat, and me being a Republican, he laughed at me. He said all us Republicans are afeared of our own shadows."

Millie walked into the building part of the restaurant to check on a few other patrons. The last voice she heard was Murray's.

"You can't drive piles into that slimy river bed and expect them to hold."

His words sent a shiver up Millie's spine. She shook it off, hoping he was one of those types that liked to complain about everything. She called them "pot stirrers" —folks that ain't happy unless everyone else is miserable too.

By the time she made her way back into the tent, the long table was empty. The men and their beer pails were gone. The only thing left was the dirty dishes and their money. Too bad, she thought. She wanted to find out more about the status of the bridge. Was that man Murray right? Was the structure around the bridge, where all those men were working, really unsafe? Alex was one of those men. She'd have to tell Connie what she overheard.

While they were washing up the lunch dishes, Millie broached the subject. She could tell by Connie's expression that it wasn't really news to her.

"Believe me, I've heard an earful from Alex already," she said. "That's all he talks about lately when he gets home."

"So you're not worried about his safety?" Sally asked, drying a plate.

"Of course, I'm worried. He's working more than one hundred feet above the river. No tellin' what might happen. He could slip and fall off without warning."

Millie tried to think of something that might help to ease Connie's worries. Nothing comforting came to mind. She couldn't tell Connie to convince her husband to quit his job. On the other hand, she couldn't tell her that everything was going to be fine. She didn't know for sure that it would be. So, she said the next best thing. "Well, you make sure you give him a big hug and kiss whenever you get the chance."

Both younger women turned and looked at Millie with scrunched up faces.

"How will that help?" Sally asked.

"At least he'll know you love him...you know, in case something does happen." Millie tried to keep the tears welling up in her eyes from spilling down her cheeks. It was a losing battle.

"Oh, I'm so sorry," Connie said, putting her arm around Millie's shoulders. "I know you miss George somethin' awful. I miss him too."

Millie walked over and unlocked the door that lead to her upstairs apartment. "I'll be right back," Millie said as she opened it. She closed the door behind her and ascended the stairs. Hearing their conversation from the kitchen, she stopped at the top step to listen.

"I never did know what happened to her husband," Sally said. "Millie just said he died and that was it...got the feelin' she didn't want to talk about it."

"She never talks about it. It was about two months ago. One

day, in the lull between the lunch and dinner crowds, I needed to walk down to Eichler's Drug Store at Tenth and Madison to get some headache medicine and, you know…something for my monthly stomach cramps. Millie decided to go with me to buy Kemp's Balsam for George's nagging cough. She's seen an ad for it in the *Enquirer*. He'd been suffering with it off and on since late February, and she was willing to try anything. So, we left George here in the restaurant alone. We weren't even gone an hour. When we got back, we found George on the floor under a ladder. He was already dead. The coroner's inquest determined he'd accidently fallen from the ladder and broken his neck…died instantly, he said."

"What was he doing on a ladder?"

"Nobody knows for sure. He had a hammer lying next to him, so they think he was fixin' something," Connie said as she pulled the stopper from sink to let the dirty wash water drain out. "Based on her advice to me just now about Alex, I'm sure Millie regrets that she never told George she loved him before she left for the drug store that day."

"How very sad," Sally said.

Millie sat on the top step for a few more minutes. She dried her tears with the edge of her apron. That dear, sweet Connie is so insightful, Millie thought. And she was right too. Millie had many regrets. She regretted that she only able to carry one baby to term after so many miscarriages. Even after William was born, she worried about him; he was so sickly all the time. She wished she had made a bigger fuss about his fifteenth birthday. She would have if she'd only known it would be his last one. She even blamed herself for William's death.

"You couldn't have known that the old mare would spook and throw him off in her panic," George had told her, trying to reassure her that it wasn't her fault. She could not have predicted how he would land or that a broken rib could do so much internal damage. None of that mattered, since it was her duty as his mother to protect him from all harm.

Her biggest regret was that she wasn't there to stop George from getting on that ladder by himself. Maybe if I had been there, he would have been more careful, she thought. Maybe I could have steadied the ladder for him or gotten whatever he needed so he wouldn't have fallen.

"Maybe..." she said softly at first, then more sternly. "Maybe I'd better get back to work."

Tuesday, June 14, 1892

The lunch rush was over; Connie and Sally were in the kitchen. Connie was washing the dirty dishes, and Sally decided to take a few minutes to eat her lunch, a ham sandwich and a small bowl of vegetable soup. Millie was in the empty dining room straightening the tables and chairs when a fancy-dressed gentleman entered.

He removed his hat with one hand and was carrying a canvas suitcase in the other. He headed for a table along the side near the window. From the window, he could see the top of the recently completed bridge pier, which stood on the Covington side of the Licking River.

"Welcome to Whitmore's," Millie greeted him and handed him a menu. "Can I get you something to drink?"

"Yes, please, some cold water," he replied, glancing down at the menu then up at Millie. "Am I too late to get your lunch special?"

Millie smiled. The menu clearly stated the specials were available between eleven in the morning to two o'clock, and the big clock on the mantel over the fireplace showed it was already a quarter past two. "I think I can manage to find one more special in the kitchen. I'll be right back."

Returning with a tall glass of iced water and a plate containing sliced ham, new potatoes and green beans, she placed them on the table in front of him. "I'll be right back with your biscuits and butter." As promised, she brought them out within a minute. "Fresh out of the oven," Millie announced as she set them down.

The man had already taken a bite of each food item and looked pleased with the outcome. "My goodness, Ma'am, I haven't tasted good ol' fashioned home cookin' since I left my mamma's back in Maryland years ago."

"Why, thank you very kindly," Millie gushed, her cheeks turning pinkish with the compliment. "Are you passing through, or are you planning to stay in the area for a while?"

The man, realizing she had seen the suitcase tucked partway under the table, replied, "I am here on business, you might say. I am James Johnson. My brother, Albert, and I left Harve de Grace, in Maryland, to go work for the Baird Brothers on a bridge being built at Hanover, Virginia. In an accident there, both of us were injured. Albert's skull was fractured, and he became a lunatic. I had to put him in an asylum. I filed a lawsuit against the contractors for $10,000 damages. Some of the money is to take care of Albert's needs, and the rest is for me, since I am unable to work due to the back injuries I sustained." He paused to eat some more of his lunch.

"I am so sorry to hear about you and your brother," Millie said sympathetically. "But how does that bring you here? If you don't mind my asking, of course."

"Oh, not at all. A friend of mine is working on the bridge here. He told me Robert Baird is here and that his brother Andrew is expected to be here tomorrow. I've come to talk to them…to see if they are willing to negotiate to settle this matter once and for all. I've just arrived in town this morning and will be staying with my friend, but he doesn't get off work until three o'clock."

Glancing at the clock at the same time, they both realized it was still at least a thirty-minute wait. "Please, take all the time you like," Millie said, then added, "Enjoy your lunch!"

"Thank you so much for your hospitality." Mr. Johnson ate the rest of his food and sipped on the water as the time slowly passed. At five minutes to three, he got up, gathered his things and left his money on the table.

Two women came in as Mr. Johnson was leaving. They selected a table in the center of the room and sat down.

"Oh, Mother, thank you so much for my wedding dress. I truly love it," the young woman said. "Are you sure the seamstress will have the alterations finished by the end of August? The wedding is on the thirty-first, you know."

"I'm paying her handsomely…she will have it done in time," the older woman replied.

Mille greeted the pair cheerfully. "Welcome to Whitmore's." She handed each them a menu. "Can I get you ladies something to drink?"

The older woman snatched the menu from her daughter and handed them both back to Millie. "We're just having some sweet tea."

"Yes, Ma'am. Two iced teas coming right up." She turned and walked to the kitchen.

As she was coming back to the table, Millie heard the young woman say, "It sure is mighty hot out, and it's only mid-June. Imagine how hot it will be in August at my wedding."

"Goodness, child, is that all you can talk about?" Her mother sounded perturbed.

Millie placed the glasses in front of the women and walked over to the table Mr. Johnson had vacated. Clearing the dishes, she overheard more of their conversation.

"No, Mother. I can talk about other things. For instance, Jack told me he's been having nightmares for the last week about that bridge. In fact, he dreamt that the whole thing fell into the river, and everyone died, including him and his two brothers. He's even thinking about quitting his job."

"He'd better not quit before finding something else first." Her mother's stern expression became more intense. "Miss Carrie Hall will not marry a vagabond!"

"He said he's only thinking about it, Mother," the young woman clarified. "Everything will be fine. In just seventy-eight days,

I will become Mrs. John Sponsor."

"But who's counting?" her mother said sarcastically, adding, "and there we have it, back to the wedding talk." She finished her tea and rose from the table, dropping a nickel as she walked away. Her daughter sheepishly followed her out.

Millie cleared the glasses and straightened up the linen table cloth for the next patrons.

Wednesday, June 15, 1892

The morning routine was exactly that –routine. Breakfast rush came and went as normal. Millie, Connie and Sally were busy cleaning up and preparing the entrees and side dishes for the next meal of the day. Around ten o'clock there was a loud crash and screaming and yelling coming from the bridge construction site. Everyone in the restaurant and the nearby houses ran to the riverbank to see what had happened.

Seeing the horrific scene, they were paralyzed with fear. Below them, between the two brick piers standing tall on each riverbank, were mounds of tangled steel, splintered wood, and mangled bodies in the river. The debris was concentrated on the Newport side. Men were swimming out to pull bodies from the muddy water.

About a hundred men were working in the rolling mill on the Covington side when they heard the crash and came running out to the scene. They too saw the workmen struggling in the water.

Twenty or so men from the Mill ran down the hillside, jumped into the river, and swam out to the wreckage. They helped a few wounded men to the river's edge, where others were waiting to get out of the water and up the incline for medical help. Next, they began the grisly business of pulling bodies out of the river and placing them on a float. Within a short time, they collected eleven bodies from the murky depths.

Connie, who had been staring down at the horror in shock,

regained her senses and ran down the hillside, calling out "Alex Thomas" the entire way. She paused just long enough to look at every wounded man who was being helped to safety. None of them was her husband.

She waited at the river's edge until the float carrying the dead reached the Covington side. Looking at each body as it was unloaded, she was relieved that Alex was not any of them. With the last body inspected, her expression immediately changed to panic. "I didn't...find Alex," she yelled breathlessly to Millie and Sally as she ascended the hill. "He must...be on...the New...port side."

Glancing down at the massive amount of debris in the river, Millie knew there was another possibility.

When Connie reached the top, she was still breathing hard, both from the physical exertion and her emotional state. "I've got...to get...to the...other...side to...find Alex."

"I can take you over," a voice in the crowd announced. Jimmie Wilson stepped forward and extended his hand to Connie to help steady herself on the ridge as she caught her breath.

Jimmie was a regular at the restaurant, and Millie had noticed that he seemed to be paying particular attention to Connie recently. Before Millie could caution her, Connie had already accepted his offer of a ride. A loud shriek ascended from the riverbank, and all eyes turned to see what it was.

A woman viewing the bodies recovered from the wreckage saw her husband and let out a blood-curdling scream as she dropped to her knees beside his lifeless form. She started crying hysterically. Two men assisted her.

Millie turned back to find Connie and Jimmie, but they were already gone. She surveyed the faces in the crowd and the variety of expressions: shock, panic, fear, curiosity, sadness, and anger. This was truly the worst disaster many of these people had ever seen.

She noticed a patrol officer standing next to a boy who couldn't have been more than seven years old. He was carrying a bucket full of coffee in one hand and a basket lunch in the other.

Tears were flowing down his cheeks. Millie walked over to them to see if she could help.

"What's the matter, lad?" Officer Donnelly asked him.

The little fellow sobbed as he explained, "I came down with lunch for my papa and my uncle, but I can't find them anywhere." He attempted to wipe his tears with the hand carrying the bucket of coffee, and spilled some on his white shirt.

His sobs were breaking the officer's heart. "What are their names?"

"My papa is Jack, I mean, John Roby, and my Uncle Billy is his brother, William Roby."

"I haven't seen them yet," Officer Donnelly said. "You'd better run on home and tell your mama what happened here. I'm sure she'll want to know."

The boy nodded his head in agreement, turned and walked away, the whole time gripping the coffee bucket and the basket holding his papa's lunch.

"Lunch!" Millie exclaimed as if she'd been startled. She suddenly realized they had left the restaurant in such a hurry, and no one was there minding the place, the food on the stove or in the ovens. She wasn't even sure how much time had passed.

She walked back to where Sally was standing, still staring down at the water. Millie touched her on the shoulder to get her attention. "I'm headed back to the restaurant. You can stay here or join me, whichever you decide."

Sally wiped a tear from her eye. "I'm going with you. Nothing I can do here, and you'll need the help, what with Connie gone for who knows how long."

Seeing smoke coming from the kitchen window could only mean one thing. The corn muffins in the oven were also a minor causality on this morning. Millie threw them out. She also dumped out the last of the coffee that had nearly evaporated away on the stove. Other than that, everything else was in good order. Not bad for being gone more than an hour, she thought.

Knowing there would be numerous people in the area, many of them ill prepared to pay for food or drinks in such a devastating situation, Millie devised a plan. She got a few pieces of paper from her desk and wrote on them. She took two biscuit baskets from the cupboard and placed one on the table nearest the front door. She placed a paper next to it that read: "During this tragedy, please take whatever food and drink you need, leave whatever payment you can."

On the door, she taped a sign that said: "Take refuge here" and below it, it said "Accepting donations for the victims and their families" She walked through the restaurant, out the side door into the tent area and over to the entrance. She placed the second basket and a duplicate paper on the table near the entrance. She pinned another sign to the tent wall at the opening.

Sally noticed what she was doing and read the paper on the table. "You're giving it away and may not even get paid for any of it. Are you crazy?"

"No, but I want to do something to help. There are a lot of people down here, some ran out of their homes and places of business without thinking about anything else. Just like we did earlier when we left food in the oven." Millie smiled, pointing to the blackened pan of muffins in the garbage pail by the back door. "I don't want anyone to go hungry or thirsty today just because they ran off without any money."

"I guess that's a nice thing to do," Sally said with a deep frown.

Millie put her arm around Sally's shoulder and squeezed it a little. "Don't worry child, I'll pay you the same as always, even if I don't make a nickel today."

Sally's whole attitude changed. "Then let's get to work," she said with as much enthusiasm as she could muster.

Whitmore's was busier than ever. Hundreds of people who had never been to the place were in and out all afternoon. Some ate a little, some just got something cold to drink, and others came in just to sit in front of a fan and let the circulating air cool them down.

Charlie took care of rushing growlers the same as any other day. A reporter from the *Enquirer* came in around two o'clock for a late lunch and an interview.

"I heard you all are doing something special here, and I wanted to find out more about it." He chatted with Millie at one of the tables while he ate his ham and soup beans, fried potatoes and cornbread muffins. "I saw the sign on your front door. What kinds of donations are you expecting to get for the victims and their families?"

Was that a hint of sarcasm in his tone? she thought.

Millie paused for a moment and then replied. "I'm sure you know it's hard on anyone to cover the expenses when someone's injured or killed on the job. No money's coming in, but there's always money going out, for things like rent, food, and medical care or funeral arrangements. Any money donated will be divided up and given to the wounded men and the families of those who died in the accident. We're also accepting clean clothes. We're giving some to the rescue workers, you know, so they can change out of their muddy and sometimes bloody clothes after they come out of the river. Also, any dressy clothes will be given to family members of the deceased for the funerals they'll be attending. Donations can be left here or at Menninger's Funeral Home."

"But the bridge construction company was insured…won't all those men will be compensated by the…"

Millie interrupted, "Sure, they may get something from the insurance…eventually. But how's that gonna help them today and tomorrow…when they got hungry babies to feed and bills to pay?" She glared at him, wondering if he'd ever experienced tragedy on a personal level. "Those of us in the community who can help must do whatever we can…it's our civic responsibility."

"I'm sorry," he said, feeling somewhat embarrassed at the way she scolded him. "I guess I wasn't thinking about that part of this whole thing."

He wrote a few notes in his journal as finished his food. Millie walked him to the door and was pleased to see him stop at the basket to drop some money into it on his way out. She watched him leave, standing in the doorway for a few minutes. She looked down towards the bridge pier and the hundreds of sightseers still gathered at the scene.

Just then, a woman about the same age as Millie ran past her towards the river. She was wringing her hands and crying, "My poor boys."

Seeing how distraught the woman was, Millie felt compelled to run after her. The woman pushed herself through the crowd and at last reached the river's edge at the base of the hillside. She was stopped by a man who knew her and knew her sons.

"You had better go back, Old Sis, you can do no good. Jack and Frank are killed, and Dick is missing," said the acquaintance.

If he had meant to tell her the information in kindness, he failed miserably. It was a cruel thing to say to her.

"My God! My darling boys are all gone now," shrieked the poor woman as she sank to the ground. She made a desperate effort to drown herself at the scene of the accident. A dozen men attempted to rescue her, but she struggled to free herself from their grasps and swim further out into the river. Finally, they managed to get her out of the water. Kind hands carried her back up the hill, and Millie directed them to take her to Whitmore's. They sat her at a table in the tent area and returned to the scene of the wreckage.

Old Sis was in shock, mumbling about her three sons.

"My oldest is Jack. He's twenty-four. Then there's Frank, just turned twenty-one. My baby boy, Dick is only eighteen. They all just started working on the bridge a week or so ago. Now they are all dead...went down with the wreck."

Jack, Frank and Dick...those names sounded familiar, Millie thought. She recalled the commotion that had taken place at the very same table just two days ago. That man named Murray Reardon was with a group of other bridge workers that included three younger men, three brothers. They were this poor woman's family.

"Please let me help you get out of those muddy, wet clothes," Millie urged. When Old Sis agreed, Millie ran upstairs to her apartment and grabbed a housedress and some undergarments. She helped her get to the bathroom to change. "You must feel like this tragedy of losing your three sons will surely be the death of you. You have to try to get through it as best you can. It will be hard, but you seem like a strong woman. Your boys would not want their deaths to cause your death too."

Old Sis gave Millie an incredulous stare. "How can you say that? You don't even know me or what I've been through."

"I've been where you are, and I survived." Millie briefly told her about William and George, and the two women cried together and hugged. She stayed with Old Sis until Officer Donnelly from Patrol 1 arrived.

"If it's okay with you, Missus Sponsor, the Chief said I can take you over to Walnut Street in Cincinnati to your friend's home."

She nodded her agreement and they left together.

The name "Sponsor" echoed in Millie's mind. She recalled the name from yesterday's encounter with the mother and daughter. Oh my heavens, she thought. That poor girl has just lost her fiancé.

During the supper rush, the only conversations to be heard were about the bridge collapse, the dead, wounded and missing workers, and who exactly was to blame for the whole thing. There was a lot of speculation and theories, Millie tried to ignore it all as she went about her business of taking orders and serving the patrons.

Sally and Charlie stayed with Millie until nearly midnight, when she finally convinced them to leave.

"You'd better get on home. I'm sure your parents are worried about you as it is…being so late and all," Millie said.

"But we can't leave you here alone," Sally protested.

"Don't worry, I'll be closing up soon. Besides, there are policemen and reporters outside so I'll be fine." She paused, thinking about all the others still milling around in the streets and along the riverbank. Then her thoughts reverted to her business. "Sally, I'll need you here at your regular time tomorrow. We've got to be open like it was any other day. People will be counting on us to give them something stable to hold on to in their crazy mixed up world. But...I don't know about Connie...if she'll be here or not."

"That's right. I've been so busy that I forgot all about...that we haven't heard anything about Alex either. What if he's hurt...or worse?" Sally gasped.

"Charlie, would you be able to come in with Sally in the morning to help with some of the breakfast chores, and maybe do some serving?"

"Sure thing, Miss Millie. I'd be happy to."

"Now that that's settled, you both run along home. And get some sleep. I'll need you both to be at your best...you know, cheerful and polite. Can't have our service lacking, especially in this time of misery and despair." She patted them lightly on the back as she let them out the back door and locked it behind them.

Thursday, June 16, 1892

Sally showed up at the back door to the kitchen at four-thirty alone. "Charlie is on the way...but he's kinda draggin' this morning," she announced. "Guess he didn't get much sleep after all. Momma said him and Daddy stayed up for hours...talking about the whole grizzly mess." She added with a little chuckle, "Probably drinking beer, too."

"Well, we'll just have to make do 'til he gets here," Millie said, picking up the coffee pot from the stove.

Sally looked at other pots and skillets full of food on the stoves. She looked in the dining room and watched Millie fill the cups of several people sitting at the tables.

When she returned to the kitchen, Sally pounced on her.

"What's going on here? What are those customers doing here this early?" Before Millie could respond, she figured it out. "Wait…you never closed up last night like you said you would."

"I didn't feel right…leaving people out in the streets and on the riverbank, still waiting for word of the missing. And if I let them in, I couldn't very well retire to my nice comfy bed upstairs knowing there were people milling about down here in my place. I just wanted to do something to help them."

"You're just the sweetest person," Sally gushed. "So caring and thoughtful about others…even total strangers."

"Well, to be honest, I can't take all the credit. I got the idea from an article I read a few years ago in *Harpers' Weekly*. It was about a flood in Pennsylvania…whole towns were destroyed. A group of volunteers showed up within a few days after the disaster to help out, you know, to provide shelter, food, clothing and money to the survivors. They had collected donations from others and didn't ask for anything in return."

"It doesn't matter where the idea came from, you were the one who put into action here."

The back door opened and Charlie strolled in. He looked better than Millie thought he would, considering how Sally had described his night.

"I'm happy you decided to join us," Millie said cheerfully. She put him to work washing dishes and other chores. Sally went out to clear tables and refill coffee cups. Morning had arrived without a sunrise. The clouds were hanging low in the river valley. Guess they were waiting more bad news too, Millie thought.

Serving food, pouring coffee and other drinks, making conversation, passing time.

Around nine thirty, there were only a couple of people left in the restaurant when the back door opened. Connie walked in, and everyone was surprised to see her.

"What are you doing here?" Millie asked. "I mean, I'm happy to see you…but I wasn't expecting you to come in today."

"I was going crazy and had to get outta there, and this is the only place I could think of to come."

"Going crazy? Why …what's happened?"

Seeing the concerned expression on Millie's face, Connie smiled, "Oh, don't worry…it's okay…"

"Wait, I want the whole story," Sally interrupted them. "You've got to tell us everything that happened after you left to go find your husband."

"Alright, alright," Connie said, "I'll start from the beginning."

When I got to the Newport side of the disaster, I asked if anyone had seen Alex Thomas. Most of the people just gave me dumbfounded looks. I must have asked twenty people before someone finally spoke up.

"I think an injured man by that name was pulled out of the river along with a few others," a man told me.

My heart must have skipped two beats…I felt faint. "Do you know what happened to him?" I asked him, frantic to find Alex. "Where did they take him?"

He said, "Cain't say fer sure, but I heard they was takin' to the boarding house up on Thornton Street." He was mumbling something else, but I was already gone…heading back up to the road to Jimmy's carriage.

"Can you take me to Thornton Street…to the boarding house? I think my husband might be there."

Jimmie nodded and off we went.

When we got to Merriweather's Boarding House, I wasn't sure what I'd find. Sure enough, Alex was there. They'd put him in one of their empty rooms. He was lying on the bed with bandages wrapped around his head. His eyes were closed, and I wasn't sure if he was alive or dead. I touched his hand, and he opened his eyes.

To my delight, he said, "Connie, is that you?"

My joy was immediately overshadowed by the wailing I

heard coming from across the hall. It was Annie Roby, Jack's wife. She was screaming hysterically. I knew her from being introduced to her on Decoration Day. Alex and I went to his friend Jack's house for a picnic. At first, I wasn't sure who she was talking to. It didn't sound like Jack.

Then I heard the man say, "Don't cry, Annie." He sounded like he was in so much pain. "Jack's all right, I hope, and I'm not going to die."

That's when I realized it was Jack's younger brother, Billy. He'd been staying with Jack and Annie for a while…until he can save enough money for his own place.

By this time, Alex was back to sleep. At least, I hoped he was sleeping. So, I went out into the hall to find the doctor or someone to tell me if Alex was going to be alright. Annie was coming out of William's room, still crying. I put my arm around her shoulders and asked how Jack was doing. Annie walked me a little way down the hall and into the next room. To my horror, there was Jack's body laid out on the bed.

Annie said to me, "Billy has a severe head injury and has been going in and out of consciousness. How can I tell him that his older brother is dead? The news would kill him on the spot." Annie wiped her eyes. "But what Billy doesn't know is that his own injuries are so frightful. A piece of timber tore most of his stomach away and the lower part of his body is paralyzed. The doctors told me he's not going to make it." Then she buried her head in my chest and sobbed uncontrollably. I didn't know what to say. I felt bad for her.

A few minutes later, a woman poked her head into the doorway and said, "Ma'am, your brother-in-law is asking for you again."

Annie grabbed my arm, urging me to go with her as she went to his bedside. I couldn't get over the sight of him, lying there in so many blood-soaked bandages."

"Don't cry, Annie. It hurts my head so," he said.

I guess she didn't want to add to his suffering, because at that moment Annie stopped crying. I left the room and went to find the doctor. At the end of the hall, I saw a man and the same woman coming out of another room.

I heard him say to a woman, "He's gone...nothing else we can do for the poor soul. Write his name on the list with the others...James. L. Johnson of Maryland." There was so much helplessness and hopelessness in his eyes.

"Are you the doctor attending to my husband, Alex Thomas?" I asked the man.

"Yes, I'm Dr. Humboldt. It appears your husband is the only one brought here this morning that may survive." His voice was so grim it gave me the shivers.

About that time, I heard Annie crying hysterically again, and I realized Billy must have died. He was my age, you know. He had his whole life ahead of him and then it was gone.

"So what happened to Alex?" Millie asked anxiously while Connie took a breath and a sip of the coffee Sally had slid in front of her while she was talking. "Is he still at Merriweather's?"

"Be patient, child," Millie said. "I'll sure she's getting to that part of the story." Millie needed a moment to come to grips with what she has just heard. Her thoughts were on the poor little fellow gripping the coffee bucket and lunch basket, looking for his father, Jack Roby and his uncle, Billy. She was also sad to hear that Mr. Johnson had the misfortune of being on the bridge when it collapsed. With him gone, she thought, who will take care of his poor brother, Albert?

"Yes, I'm getting to it," Connie said, then she swallowed a few more sips of coffee before going right back into her story-telling mode.

Oh, no, thank goodness. Alex was at Merriweather's for several hours before Dr. Humboldt finally said he could leave. He'd sent a boy around the corner to get some pain medicine for him. He wrote out some instructions for me...you know, how to give him the medicine. He also wrote out to let him sleep for no more than an hour at a time, then wake him up and talk to him. He said brain injuries were tricky business.

He wanted me to ask him questions to make sure he knew things. The doctor was worried his head injury might be worse on the inside than what it appeared on the outside. Actually we ended up staying the night at the in-laws. Alex's mother insisted on it once she heard the instructions. She especially didn't like the part about if he didn't wake up or if he did know the right answers, we had to take him to the hospital right away.

She told me, "You'll need help making sure Alex wakes up good through the night."

"She was right too. By eleven o'clock, I was exhausted.

His mother said, "Go get some sleep...I'll take care of my son."

I was too tired to argue with her. But I did ask her to wake me if anything happened. Next thing I knew, it was morning, and she was making breakfast. I asked her, "Why didn't you wake me up to take over the next watch?"

She told me, "You were sleeping so soundly, I didn't have the heart to wake you." Then she added, "Besides, I wouldn't have been able to sleep knowin' my baby was in harm's way."

That was a mean thing for her to say. As if I didn't care about him as much as she did. She handed me a cup of coffee, smiling that smile of hers...you know, the one that says, "he may have married you, but I'll always be his ever-lovin' momma." Well, I had to leave her kitchen before I said something back at her that I might regret. I went in to check on Alex, and he looked fine…sounded fine too."

"Momma is making me her special scrambled eggs…just like she used to when I was a little boy." He sounded like a little boy again, it was eerie.

That was about all I could take. I told Alex that I needed to go to work and tell you how he was doing…you know, so you all wouldn't worry. And I told him I wanted to see if there was anything I could do to help out. I had heard there were still hundreds of people on the riverbank, watching them pulling debris and bodies from the river and waiting for word about their missing loved ones.

"So here I am," Connie said, spreading her arms open wide, "and now you're all caught up."

"Well, I am so glad Alex is alright." Sally said, giving Connie a hug. "And I'm glad you're here. Yesterday was crazy, and it will probably be the same today…that is, until they announce all the workers have been accounted for…you know, one way or another." The grim reality of that statement turned her smile into a frown.

"I'm glad everything's fine with Alex too," Millie added, knowing there were a lot of people who could not say the same thing this morning.

Monday, December 19, 1892

Millie finished her morning chores with a few minutes to spare before opening the restaurant for the breakfast crowd. She was alone as she had been the last couple of weeks. Sally and Charlie had stopped working back in September once school started up again.

Connie gave her notice and stopped working right before Thanksgiving. She'd already gained about twenty pounds even though she was only in her fifth month. Someone had joked about the possibility of twins, and she nearly had a heart attack. Since she was having difficulty maneuvering around the tables, especially with her ankles beginning to swell, she decided it was time to make good on her promise to quit and stay home to have and raise her family.

Alex was fully recovered from his head injury, and even the nightmares were becoming less frequent. During the five weeks following the bridge collapse, both Coroner Wilson of Kenton County and Coroner Davis of Campbell County conducted separate investigations. They both concluded the contractors, Robert and Andrew Baird, who perished in the accident along with their men, were not at fault.

They found no evidence of shoddy workmanship on the bridge or the false work. Complaints that the overall bridge design was flawed, which made the collapse inevitable, were disproven. Even the claims that defective or "second-hand" timbers were being used could not be proven. Thirty-one men died, and more than twenty were injured on that fateful day.

With the bridge company's contractors exonerated of any wrongdoing, the insurance company reluctantly settled with the victims' families. Alex used some of his settlement money to pay the tuition at Nelson Business College so he could become an accountant.

Sipping her coffee, Millie picked up the *Enquirer* and flipped through the pages, reading the headlines. On page two, at the very bottom of the page, a small article caught her eye. The headline read, "The New Bridge Opened." The article said the beautiful new structure spanning the Licking River opened to the public yesterday, apparently with little fanfare or publicity.

It said there will be no restriction on the driving of horses, or fast trotting, across the bridge, since it was built with rapid transit in mind. It also mentioned the inclusion of electric street railway lines across the bridge which were expected in the coming year.

PARENTS ARE THE BEST TEACHERS
by Alvena Stanfield

If we could see ourselves through our children's eyes we would find praise, encouragement and interest in them acquiring new skills decline as the child advances beyond toddler. Once a child learns to talk parents slide away, depending more on Kindles, video games, television and smart phones. If you think this writer is wrong, look around at a kid's favorite restaurant.

Instead of using this time to praise, encourage and increase good relationships the parents are texting or chatting, but not with the little person sitting across from them . Occasionally they do talk with the child. Sentences are short. "Eat your fries." "Stop making a mess." "Quit nudging your brother," and "Hurry up."

We tell ourselves we are too busy. But underneath this inattention is the philosophy that beyond age five, our children don't need us to nurture them. The reverse is true. A charming toddler who falls and cries will find several hands reach out, pick him up, comfort him and help him acquire balance. But when an eight year old struggles with reading, math, bullying or social growth he finds himself alone, sitting across from a parent who prefers to text, criticize or talk with someone else.

We parents are our children's first teachers. The Northern Kentucky Education Council and our public schools have statistically proven a half hour spent with an adult giving undivided attention to a struggling reader or math student can reverse illiteracy. We volunteers within this program lavish praise and encouragement along with making learning fun for only a half hour a week. This child's parent, as his or her first and lifelong teacher, is more important and can enrich their child better with a half hour a week of reading or playing games with them.

For three years every child this writer spent a half hour a week with has become proficient. The magic? No. Simple games, reading with them and most of all praise are the only magic. I love sharing. Call me at 859-409-3434 or email to stanfieldwrites@gmail.com if you are interested in trying these simple games.

DAMSELS IN DISTRESS
by Leslie Bush

Chapter 1

A young man stood straight with his head held high. A long black cloak with a fine silver lining swirled around his black clad body. Hair, blacker than the deepest void, fell into his pale, noble face. His long fingered hand lay on the ornate pommel of a silver sword. With his ebony eyes focused forward, he stepped out into the busy street and right into a fresh pile of horse droppings. Flaring his arms, he unsuccessfully tried to catch his balance and fell backwards with a splatter.

With skillful, agile movements, a petite elvish woman, dressed in a forest green suit, bounced out of the way of the flying filth. A frown crossed her pouting, full, red lips. Her features relaxed, and mischief lit her blue eyes. Puffing her jaws with air, she had to let it go with a full laughter.

"That's no way to impress a potential employer, Shadow," she remarked once she caught her breath.

Frowning, Shadow looked up at the woman from his sitting position. He gave her a glare that would wither the strongest of weeds. "Oh, do be quiet, Pixel! At least, I am seeking legitimate employment."

Crossing her arms, Pixel only stood on the sidewalk. A smirk twitched her jaw. "I do well enough," she remarked, as she adjusted the jingling purse at her slender waist.

Shaking his head, Shadow pulled himself up to his feet. Folding his hands with the index fingers to his thin lips, he closed his eyes in concentration. A blacklight encased his form. The filth upon his clothes and body slid away to the street. The corners of his mouth quirked up in a smile at his success. Opening his eyes, he lowered his hands.

The filth that had left him continued to glow black. It oozed into the street and combined with more foul smelling dirt. An amorphous mass formed and swirled. With a loud crack like thunder, the dirt exploded into unnatural black flames. Wafts of acrid stench filled the air.

Shadow's face turned a shade paler. Taking Pixel's hand from her giggling mouth, he pulled her across the street. A welcoming doorway to a tavern beckoned the fugitives away from the glares of the people in the street. Hurriedly, Shadow pushed Pixel into the establishment and followed himself. Smoothing down his clothes, he stood up straight and raised a hand.

"Hi there, guys!" he announced, as he strutted casually to a booth table.

Adjusting the bow on her back, Pixel followed him. Her wide eyes took in the dress of these people and the size of the purses at their belts. Given that most of the people here were of the male persuasion, she was certain that her innocent appearance would pay off well. Many of the patrons would leave here with a lot less coins and possessions.

A shapely barmaid, with more-than-a-little revealing uniform on her robust form, approached their table. Shadow's dark eyes took in every inch of her curves and showcased bosom. A toothy smile, showing off his longer than normal canine teeth, crossed his mouth. The sharp pain in his foot, delivered by his scowling companion, reminded him of his purpose here.

"Give me a pin of beer, and she'll have. . .a. . .uh. . ." he ordered, as he eyed his small companion, who had the appearance of an eight-year-old. "Give her a glass of milk."

Pixel gave him a firm kick under the table. Making firm contact, she smiled as Shadow's cheeks turned purple and sat up rigidly straight. After a moment, he slumped in his seat.

The barmaid snorted and walked away. She returned with the items ordered. After she placed the drinks on the table, she held out her hand for payment.

Puzzlement crossed Shadow's face, then realization lit his eyes. He dug through his clothes without success. Sitting up he snapped his fingers and produced a purse from the air. Sighing with relief, he opened it. His face fell, as he emptied it out on the table. A ball of string, a rock, and a crumpled piece of paper with I.O.U. written on it fell out.

The barmaid frowned. "If you can't pay, Brutus and Bruiser will take pleasure in taking payment out of you," she remarked, as she nodded to the two sizeable trolls at the bar.

"Uh . . . Pixel?" he requested.

The elven girl sighed and shook her head. Pouring out a couple of coins in her hand, she gave the barmaid the payment. Satisfied, the barmaid walked away, and Shadow let out a held breath.

"Shadow, I didn't choose to travel with you so that you could spend my funds."

"What are you complaining about? You just recently lifted those coins from someone in town."

"That's my business, not yours!" she spat back.

Holding up his hands, he objected. "I'm trying to find work! Why do you think we're in this tavern?"

"Trying to hide from the people, who noticed that stinky spell of yours," she returned cattily.

"Hmpf!" he returned, as he narrowed his eyes at her.

A normal person would have felt a cold chill run down the spine. Pixel only smirked at him.

"Taverns are places," he said, "where the town socializes. If there is any work to be had, it will be spoken of here."

Pixel snorted. With a swift movement, she snatched the mug of beer.

"Hey! Wait a moment! That's mine!" he complained.

"Yeah? Who paid for it?" she returned, as she downed the drink. "Despite appearances, I'm older than you. You can have the milk."

Crossing his arms, he gave up and leaned back into the dark corner of the booth.

Different colored lights lit up the stage at the far corner of the tavern. A blue-haired half elf of a wiry and extraordinarily limber build jumped out on the stage. His fingers danced up and down on a tortured, splinter-worn, but brightly painted, guitar. Those, who were familiar with the genre called metal, may have referred to this as shredding and would have been impressed if the half elf had not been tone deaf. The lanterns around the stage cast different colors upon his rainbow, ragged clothes. Unfortunately, the effect was not what the musician had intended; instead of being inspirational, it looked more like someone had puked on his clothes. The foul smoke coming from his thin cigarette surrounded him like a psychedelic halo.

"Hey there all,
Listen to my groovy, far out song!
The Grateful Dead Dude
Rides again.
You see, he got himself a wow woman.
Dragged her down that rabbit hole of his,
And covered her in muck and mud,
And did other things, best not mentioned, to her.
She said, "Way out, Man!"
Till I invited myself along.
That's when the whips and chains came out!"

Several people gagged, and dishes of food were thrown towards the stage. Several cat calls of less than a savory nature were yelled out. Shadow was not sure that Pixel was old enough to be exposed to such things. Scratching his head, he was not sure he was old enough himself.

Voices came from the booth behind them. Waving his hands to hush his gagging companion, he cocked his head. Furrowing his brow, he listened closer to the conversation held.

"Was it really a good idea to bring Kel along with us, Nikodemus?" asked the voice of a young man.

"You know Kel, Tallon. He comes and goes where he pleases," answered a somewhat high-pitched voice.

"Nothing is right with this world!" complained Tallon. "It seems wherever we are, Kel shows up. Then, there is a princess stuck in that gloomy Castle of Golzeckia with that undead necromancer!"

"And what are you going to do about it, my boy?"

"Hmpf! Nothing. I have enough woman problems as it is without risking my life and sticking my nose in their business!"

Jumping up from the table, Shadow took hold of Pixel's wrist and pulled her from the tavern. He had found his job!

A small, dark elven figure, dressed in an oversized white t-shirt and blue jeans, bounced out of the booth to watch the departing couple. A wide smile crossed his jovial face.

"Another sucker drawn in," he commented.

A young man in a simple tunic stood behind the elvish figure. "You make more work for me than any apprentice should have to endure!"

Chapter 2

A lean man sat back in a comfortable armchair by a crackling fire. His dark hair was combed neatly back from his noble, finely chiseled face. Gray streaks in the black hair suggested that he had lived longer than his youthful, blue eyes would suggest. The dark velvet suit accented his muscular build without bragging. The sword at his side was not overly fancy and was more for utility than show . .

. a well-balanced weapon that had seen its fair share of battles. Holding a goblet of brandy in his right hand, the man leaned on his left and watched the flickering fire.

The ominous slam of the heavy oaken door broke his concentration.

A hunched, cloaked figure scurried into the room. Shaking himself like a dog, the figure threw off the clinging rain water. Throwing back his hood, he revealed the long, stringy hair that framed his round head. Lifting his head with a show of his buck teeth, he scanned the room for signs of other intruders with beady, dark eyes. Twitching his rather large, round ears, he searched for any sound out of the ordinary. Scratching the scraggily stubble of a beard around his jaw, he twitched his pointed nose. Without further ado, the figure made his way to the table at the noble man's side and took up the decanter of brandy. Without a word, he downed the entirety of the contents.

"Ever heard of using a glass, Roland?" the seated man asked calmly.

Roland belched as a response, then wiped his mouth on his sleeve. Distant thunder filled the room. Twitching and crouching low, he looked around the room to make sure everything was still sound. With a nod of satisfaction, he made his way in front of the regal man. Standing up straight, he rummaged through his cloak to produce a package. Hurriedly, he gave it to the seated man.

"Snatched it from the carrier this morning, I did, Lord Valerius," he announced.

Frowning, Valerius looked the package over. "You needn't steal from the carrier, you know. Thievery is not a good thing." With a bit more inspection, Valerius sighed and placed the package on the table at his side. "It's from Marissa," he remarked. "What a strange woman my sister is! I miss her wedding, and she sends me a present. I will call my wizards in later to check the package for booby traps. Alas! That will be awhile. They are all off on special missions now."

A commotion occurred at the door. Roland jumped a good foot

off the floor, looked around frantically, then hid behind the lord's chair. Valerius remained unmoved, as two young people rushed into his presence. Two guards with neat, dark brown uniforms followed them. Both guards seemed drenched in slime and had glowing, white slugs on their shoulders. Each guard grabbed an intruder. The petite female captive back kicked her captor in a delicate place. The man doubled over. The dark man captive expertly twisted his way out of the grip of the other guard and ran to his counterpart, encircling her protectively with his arms.

"Do you know who I am?" the young man demanded. Dumbfounded, the guards looked at each other and shrugged. "I am Shadowmance, the fantastic wizard of Lycel, and this is my most esteemed traveling companion, Pixel."

"Yeah, it's a fantasy on his part," she smirked, as she wiggled her way out of his embrace.

Valerius stood up from his chair. "Leave them," he ordered. "Roland is here with me, and I am not defenseless on my own."

The guards looked at each other. With a shrug, they left the room, as they casually tried to knock the slugs off their shoulders.

Straightening his ruffled clothes, Shadow stepped forward and made a bow. "Thank you, good sir. I was told you could be of service to us. Word on the street is that you are a nobleman, come here to do righteous deeds."

"That's the cleaned up, nice version of it," Pixel remarked. "It was more like you were a vile, busybody who came to town with highfalutin ideas and soon would find yourself in a big rat trap."

Shadow's eyes opened wide, and he slapped a hand around the small woman's mouth. He looked to the master of the house and gave a lopsided grin.

"Tell me what you wish of me," Valerius told them.

"I am new to town. My companion and I have been traveling town to town to sharpen our skills and make a name for ourselves," Shadow explained. Stomping Pixel's foot, he sent her a vile glare before she could make another comment. "I have heard tell of a princess, being held by an evil sorcerer. My colleague and I want to retrieve this maiden before unspeakable things befall her."

"Personally, I couldn't care less," grumbled Pixel.

Meanwhile, Roland feeling that the danger had passed, crept out from behind the chair. The mysterious package on the table called to him like a siren in the vast ocean. Creeping up on it, he poked at it. Since he didn't lose a digit nor did the package make any kind of warning noise or movement, he braved in a bit closer. Giving a quick glance to the master of the house, he assured himself of the safety of the venture. Snatching the box, he shot back to his hiding place.

Satisfied that the master was properly otherwise occupied, he shook the box. It only gave a dull rattle but nothing more. Dealing with all the subdued curiosity that he could muster, Roland carefully pulled the strings, holding the box together. Listening closely and sniffing the air for any scent of danger, like explosive powder, he cautiously took hold of the lid with deleterious, little hands. With a surge of courage, he pulled it away. His beady eyes grew wide at the sight of the contents.

"They're almond cookies! My favorite!" he exclaimed, as he picked one up.

Alerted to his servant's illicit activities, Valerius rose from his chair and hit him with a fair force. Roland fell forward and dropped the cookie. "They're not yours! You know better!" he reprimanded him.

"But you share everything with me anyway. You say sharing will make the world a better place, and there'd be no need for thievery. Of course, I would be out of a job, if that happened," complained Roland.

"Think, Roland. Cookies from my sister may not be the best thing to put in your mouth."

"Ah, but sir, they don't look so burnt this time. Smell it a bit, but I've eaten worse," the little man argued.

"It's not her ability to cook. It's those special ingredients she's so fond of using."

Roland dropped the box as quick as the snap of a rat trap. Shadow raised an eyebrow and moved to clean it up, but Valerius held up a hand to stop him. Roland snorted, and pulling out a pair of special gloves, he put them on and cleaned up the mess. Fetching a broom and dustpan, he gathered up the crumbs.

"Marissa's cookies can be caustic to the flesh," Valerius explained.

"Oh," answered Shadow.

"Tell me more of this princess and this sinister ploy that holds her captive," Valerius urged him.

"She is being held at the castle of Golzeckia," Shadow told him.

"Hmm. I know the place. It is a truly wicked place, full of the vilest monster ever to tread Amgen. Strange. I thought a couple of my friends had cleaned out the place and defeated the evil lord." Stroking his chin in thought, he watched Roland clean up the spilt cookies. "Yes, I think I have time for this side project. I would very much like to know what happened to my friends, who went there. How do you feel about an adventure, Roly?"

Roland jumped visibly at the suggestion. Having swept up the cookies into the dustpan, he dumped them into the fireplace. An explosion burst forth and threatened to break from the hearth. After a moment, the fire settled back down into a comfortable crackle. Satisfied, Roland threw his gloves into the flames. Silently, he made his way to the liquor cabinet and pulled forth another decanter of brandy. After he poured the liquor on each palm to clean away any residue of the tainted gift, he took a swig from the bottle for good measure. Feeling a bit more relaxed, he turned to his master and his request.

"Well, . . . uh, sir. I do have some things to attend to, you know. The missus, she has been chewing at me something awful about spending time with the litter and all."

"Ah! Excellent! Then you will be here to track down the leader of the Black Mark for me! Good man! I could entrust such a delicate or such a dangerous task to no one else."

"Uh . . . ," responded Roland, as he stood up straight and scratched the back of his head. "Yeah, well, you know. The missus, she's been on her own for some time now, and you may need my expertise."

"Alright, then! We're set. Let's go clean out the bad guys!" exclaimed Valerius with more enthusiasm than necessary.

Shadow and Pixel looked at each other with puzzlement. Pixel slapped her partner hard.

"What kind of trouble have you gotten me into this time, you idiot!"

Chapter 3

With the enthusiasm of a ten-year old boy going on a fishing trip, Valerius led his companions to the stables. Shrugging, Shadow followed. Pixel sighed and threw up her hands. Roland brought up the rear in a much slower stagger. In his hands, he held a golden bauble that he had acquired from Shadow's purse. Several sparkly things swirled around inside, and he could not take his eyes from it. Rolling it back and forth from hand to hand, he watched the twinkling lights caught in the surface. Suddenly, a snap like the spring of a rat trap and a flash of light came from it. With a yelp, Roland dropped his prize. The bauble floated a moment on its own. With a blur, it flew back into Shadow's purse. The wizard turned to look at the thieving servant. His dark eyes twinkled evilly from the shadows of his brow. Roland swallowed hard and took a step back.

Oblivious, Valerius entered the stables. His stride became more determined at the sight of a black mare in a stall. He went to her and placed his hand upon her nose. A wide smile crossed his lips. The horse whinnied and cuddled his hand.

"How have you been, my dear Pansy. Yes, yes. We are heading out for another adventure to set the world to rights. Are you as excited as I am?"

The horse neighed loudly. Pulling back, she shook her head and pawed the ground. A luxurious mane flowed around her fine, graceful neck. Setting his fists upon his hips, Valerius stood up straight. "I thought as much."

With a motion to the two stable hands, Valerius ordered them to gather supplies. From the corner, where they were playing dice, they gave him a brief glance. With a snort, they returned to their game. Roland scurried behind his master and looked to the non-responsive servants. With a nod, he made his way to their corner. Chattering a strange, high pitched language, he caught the two's attention. He ended his speech with what sounded like "Meow! Meow!" The two sat up straight as if they had been struck by lightning. With wide eyes, they looked to Valerius. Swallowing hard, they pocketed the dice and jumped up to do the master's bidding.

"What did you say to them?" Shadow asked.

"Ah," answered the little man, as he pulled at his collar. "I just told them they could do what the master asked, or he would bring his collection of stray cats from Talamar to come live here with him in Shady Valley."

Pixel and Shadow looked at each other. An icy chill ran down each of their spines. "All right," Pixel answered slowly. "The sooner we leave this sludge hole, the better."

Valerius danced happily around the stables and chose the proper mounts for his companions. Judging Pixel's size, he chose a pony for her. Roland received a pony of a similar size. Shadow got saddled with an old nag, who chewed a cud fiercer than any cow ever had.

Standing by the haggard animal, Valerius nodded to Shadow. "We are short on horses, because many of my men are out on special business. Patricia may not look it, but she is a sturdy, steadfast animal."

Looking around at the stable, Shadow saw no other full-sized horse available. Swallowing hard, he reached out to pet the beast. She snapped at him with the speed of a cat on its prey. Since he was used to such violent actions from his traveling companion, he successfully jumped away.

Pixel stood back with crossed arms in silence for a moment with an expressionless face. A twitch jerked her lip. She was able to keep her composure for a few more moments. Finally, wrapping her arms around her belly, she let go a full laughter.

"Shut up!" ordered Shadow. "Or else I will turn you into the toad you are."

"I would likely become a queen with the way your magic works," she smirked once she caught her breath.

"Now! No fighting, friends. We have a princess to rescue!" reprimanded Valerius, as he adjusted his sword. "Roland, go fetch that bag of special herbs. You know the one. It's the one that I got from Kel. You'll have to snatch it away from the kitchen servants, but Patricia needs it more than they do."

With a nod, Roland ran off to do what he was told. He returned with a blue bag with a strange symbol on it. The symbol looked like a turkey foot in a circle. He pulled out a handful of what looked to be dried weeds and held it out to the horse. She snarled at him and his offering. She spat out her cud at him. Roland stood his ground. Cautiously, the horse sniffed at the plant. With a snort, she began to eat it. Soon the handful and the rest in the bag were gone. After a few minutes of digestion, her eyes glazed over, and a look of euphoria overtook her features. She staggered in place like an undulating wave. She nosed Shadow with a soft whinny.

The wizard lifted his lip in disgust. Pixel fell to the ground in a hard laughter. With a sigh, Shadow gave in and mounted the now happy horse. Regaining control of herself, Pixel mounted her pony and cantered out. With a shake of his head, Shadow tried to maneuver his horse left, then right, maybe a straight line. After several minutes, he managed to adjust to the commands needed for this mellow steed to get her to move forward.

After donning his shining armor, Valerius was ready for action. He led the group out of his home and into the streets of Shady Valley. They passed through the clean, up kept part of town straight into the dark, narrow streets, where the smell of urine and blood permeated the air. Several ladies of questionable professions waved at them. Some of these ladies ran to the men and affectionately stoked their backs and thighs. A woman even tried to entice Pixel. With narrow eyes, Pixel drew her dagger on her assailant and reclaimed her purse from the thief. The harlot left with a huff.

Once the ladies dispersed to their separate haunts, Roland disappeared from his horse. His clothes fell in a silent testament of his once being there. The clothing shuffled a bit, and a large black rat surfaced. It jumped from the saddle. Several minutes passed with the servant's absence, but Valerius seemed unconcerned. He didn't even seem to notice. The rat scurried around the street and disappeared into black holes, then resurfaced to do it all again. Finally, the rat jumped from corner to corner of the surrounding, shabby buildings to land in the clothes again. A sack almost as big as itself was in its mouth. It nosed its way back into the clothes, and within moments, Roland reappeared as if nothing had happened. Whistling, he delved into the impossibly deep bag and produced a change purse. This he threw to Valerius. In a similar way, he returned the stolen goods to Shadow. Catching a different —and previously invisible— purse in his delicate hands, he tied it to his belt.

"Thank you, my good man," Valerius told him with a pat on the head. Bending over backwards, he opened one of his saddle bags. With a small effort, he pulled forth a greasy, brown sack and handed it over to his companion. "For a job well done."

"Thank you, master! Cooked potato shavings! My favorite! They even have extra oil! You're the best master any being could ask for!"

Soon they exited the town and came upon the opened road. The sun was bright and a few puffy clouds played along the blue sky. Valerius looked up at the sky and smiled. "Come now, my good companions. I say we need a round of song to keep our pace. It will be a good, hard day's journey to get to Gozleckia. Song is good for the morale. It will help us along the treacherous road ahead."

Pixel and Shadow looked to each other. Shadow's horse

staggered.

"Roland, you want to start us off with a good song?" Valerius offered.

"Uh, sir. You've never asked before," the small man replied, as he licked the grease from his fingers. "You always said my songs were buggers. Thought them quite good, personally."

"Yeah, uhm," muttered Valerius. "That song about Lady Mable and her activities under the table was not exactly proper for the ladies of Talamar. Looking around to his other two companions, he shrugged off the redness in his cheeks.

"How about I sing us a song?

"Gone are doubts and fears, there's nothing holding us back
From crushing all who stand against the power and the might
Of brethren, such us as we, who bring the glory and the law.
They fall beneath our banners as we charge with holy light.

Treading fearless forward to the place where evil dwells,
Trusting in the good that conquers all the wicked in the end,
Crash the gates and burn the towers, voices crying out
For justice and for freedom, for the righteous we defend.

Horses thunder onward with the ringing of our swords,
Swifter than the wind, we ride against the coming storm.
Through the thunder and the lightning, all our battles won,
Standing high forever with the ringing of our horns."

Shadow's horse whinnied and stomped her feet in a disorientated dance.

Looking sidelong to her companion, Pixel asked loudly for all to hear, "Are you sure that getting this guy was such a good idea?"

Pulling the reins tight, Shadow struggled to regain control of his horse. "It's better than going at it alone, and he didn't charge any kind of fee."

"You get what you pay for," she muttered.

"Come on. One more round of song!" Valerius encouraged.

"I think I'm going to stuff him!" grumbled Pixel.

"It's not that bad. He could have the singing voice of that bard in town."

Noticing that his companions were falling behind, Valerius cried out to them. "Come on! No slacking! That princess is awaiting us!"

Pixel spat an unladylike comment. Shadow turned an entertaining shade of red. Oblivious to her meaning, Valerius continued forward. Roland rode up beside her with a wicked grin.

"I know a private, little hole where we can test such things out," he offered brightly.

Narrowing her eyes, Pixel turned her glare upon the ratty man. Roland swallowed hard, and the smile disappeared from his face. With a forced grin, he stopped his horse, and without another word, he allowed her to move forward.

"Look!" cried out Valerius as he pointed ahead. "There it is on the horizon! The castle of Gozleckia!"

They rode up a steep hill and looked out over the horizon. In the distance, a dark, foreboding, squat structure sprawled out like a brooding spider awaiting its prey.

"And I'm coming along for this . . ." muttered Pixel. "There had better be riches beyond imagine there, or else you will never spawn children!"

Shadow turned pale.

Chapter 4

As night set in, Valerius called for them to pitch camp. Roland happily left the group and gathered wood for the campfire. Soon, Valerius had a cheery blaze burning. Smiling, he pulled a bag from his sack. Digging deep into the bag, he produced a soft, puffy, white object. It was large enough that one could not swallow it whole, but it was small enough that it made a nice handful.

"Take one, and get a stick to spear it with," he told the others, as he passed the sack around.

Pixel took a spongy thing from the bag and looked at it with puzzlement. "What's this?"

"They are called marshmallows," Valerius explained. "I have a friend who does a bit of dimensional travel, and he brought me back this sack. They are quite edible and even better when toasted. No campfire is complete without them. So, take up a stick and join me."

Shadow shrugged and stuck the gooey sweets on the end of the stick like Valerius did. "You should have brought this wizard friend with you on this venture. Undead wizards are not easily defeated."

"Ah, we'll be alright," Valerius assured him. "We have the will of Eleysius, the god of the righteous, on our side."

After a round of scary stories from the menfolk, the party curled up in their separate places to sleep. Roland made an offer to keep Pixel especially warm. Shadow knew better, and Valerius was too much of a gentleman. Squeaking and squealing, Roland left Pixel's tent. His hands covered his privates as he fled for a safer haven. With no further ado, they all settled down to sleep without further incident.

As the sun peaked over the horizon, the party awoke and prepared for their adventure. Shadow gave his horse that special feed, and they set out again. As they descended into the valley, Shadow and Pixel surveyed their surroundings. Roland surveyed the fine curves in front of him. If Pixel was aware of his scrutiny, she would have insisted upon him riding up front with his master.

Shadow opened his eyes wide at the sight of the countryside around him and looked down at Pixel. The little elf shared a similar look of confusion.

A castle of a vile, heinous wizard should have a treacherous road with thorny briars and vile, dark things lurking in the shadows. This was the standard that every child was taught for these kinds of stories. The road to Gozleckia was well kept and paved. The grass was a little tall, but it was of a reasonable height. It could hide small animals, but nothing large and foreboding lurked there. The bright, blue sky above with the casually floating clouds did nothing to set the proper scene.

"I thought there would be perpetual storm clouds and lightning around evil places," Shadow complained.

"Ah, my dear Shadow, no one knows where evil lurks. We must always be on guard from such malignance. What better disguise for its true intent than sunny skies can it have?" Valerius remarked.

"The same can be said about dingleberries," Pixel added.

"Do dingleberries taste good?" piped Roland.

After a couple of hours of travel and Valerius' enthusiastic singing, they finally came to the moat around the castle. No stench raised up from the water. No muck lapped up the banks. No monster surfaced in the water. Actually, the water was crystal clear. Several rather large orange fish with black and white freckles and little whiskers swam to the surface to greet the newcomers. Laughing, Valerius reached into his saddle bags and pulled forth a sack of bread crumbs.

"Come on. I have plenty and some to spare," he told the fish as he spread the bread crumbs out.

The fish eagerly fought to see who could get to the feed first. Several jumped out of the water, spraying the air with sparkles like pixie dust.

Shadow, Pixel and Roland watched with arms crossed.

A creak, then a slam of the wooden drawbridge scattered the fish and caught the attention of all four of the company. Roland had to excuse himself for a change of pants. Shadow and Pixel both raised eyebrows. With a wave of his hand, Shadow cast a spell. Several silver insects crawled over the edge of the bridge. Flicking their antennae, the insects moved along the surface and left a thick silver slime behind them.

Closing his eyes, Shadow concentrated. His cheeks turned red and sweat beaded his forehead, as he opened his eyes. "Well," he remarked, "It sort of worked. There are no traps on the bridge."

Turning to Roland, who had returned and was adjusting his clean pants, Valerius ordered. "Let the horses go and graze."

"Yes, sir," the little man replied. "And should I stay behind and guard them? Never know what kind of ruffians may be lurking about, sir."

"That is a great idea!" Valerius told him. "You can entertain that black cat I saw lurking around."

"Uh, sir. I think things are safe here. The wizard discovered no traps, nor have I seen any signs of trickery. The horses will be fine. I think I'll go with you to protect you, Master."

Roland danced along the bridge. His feet barely touched the surface, as he passed. Pixel followed him in a less hurried pace, but she was too avoided the slimy muck left behind by the insects. The two remaining men looked at each other a moment. Valerius, being the more brave of the heart, went first. For a while, he managed to step around the mess. With each step, he gained confidence. Looking back at Shadow, he motioned for him to follow. It was then that he stepped in a large, thick puddle. Flaring his arms, he muttered several words that no virtuous man should know, much less say in mixed company. Falling backwards, he shifted his weight forward. It worked for a moment, but he continued to fall forward. He landed face down in the muck. The force of his weight propelled him forward into his two waiting companions. Without a word, Roland helped the knight to his feet.

Upon seeing his companion's less than graceful entrance, Shadow chose to cast another spell. Folding his hands and closing his eyes, he concentrated upon the power within. The wind whipped around him and picked him up. With a little more concentration, he levitated to the wooden planks of the bridge. A smug smile crossed his face as he felt success within his grasp. Then the spell let go. The wizard's body jerked with the sudden freedom, and he hit the surface with a sickening splat. Unlike Valerius, his propelled motion sent him over the edge into the moat. Grumbling, he surfaced in the water and swam to the shore. With a helpful hand, Valerius pulled him up to join the group.

Pixel only laughed and moved into the shadows of the doorway. Roland, likewise, disappeared into the darkness. Valerius and a dripping Shadow boldly walked forward. None of them seemed to care about what was going on behind them on the bridge.

Once all the traffic was gone, several skeletons, wearing smocks and carrying brooms, mops and buckets appeared from nowhere. Normally, such an unnatural occurrence would have been unnerving, but no one of importance saw them. They proceeded to clean away the goop left behind by the uninvited visitors. A sizeable, black house cat, ignoring these undead minions, bounced across the causeway.

The four adventurers entered the courtyard and were struck dumb by its appearance. The grass and greenery were well trimmed and healthy. Several flowers of various colors and breeds were spotted throughout the garden. Even an herb garden with little identifying signs nestled itself against the wall. A statue of a tall man in exquisite clothes stood in the middle of the yard. He held up one hand, where crystal water flowed outward and down to the basin at his feet. In his right hand was a staff with a skull atop it. At his feet were various bone remains of his victims. In the basin was the clear, clean water. Not a ripple disturbed the water, as several round, orange and white fish waddled around lazily.

Shadow's shoulders tensed, and he touched his sword as he looked around. Moving among the greenery were several decaying zombies. They shuffled around the garden tending to it with the proper tools. None of these undead beings carried any of the conventional weapons. They had shovels, rakes, hoes, and shears. If a chunk of rot fell from their bodies, and it often did, they would work it into the soil to feed the plants.

A glimpse of white caught the attention of the living. Several skeletons, dressed in the same simple smocks as those on the bridge, hurried around the premises. Each of them carried cleaning material of one kind or another. Some had brooms and swept the walks.

Others had cloths with which they cleaned the pristine windows. None of the undead seemed to pay any attention to the intruders.

Fear soon dissipated, and even Roland jumped down from under Valerius' cloak. The little man stood crouched for a little longer, but he soon relaxed. Shadow stood up straight and looked down at Pixel. Scratching his head, he furrowed his brow. The little woman shared his confusion.

Without fear, Valerius stepped forward to the main path leading to the door. One of the skeletons approached him with a bucket and a cloth. At first, the warrior wanted to draw his sword and put down this undead atrocity, but the skeleton made no aggressive move. It diligently cleaned away the muck on the man's armor.

Shaking off the strange scene, Roland returned to his instincts. Rolling up his sleeves, he flexed his delicate fingers. Hopping onto the ledge of the fountain, he reached into the water to catch one of the roly-poly fish. Before his fingers could wrap around his prey, his dark, beady eyes met with the large green eyes of a black cat.

"Meow?" the cat spoke casually.

"Eek!" screamed Roland, and he returned to his place under the master's cloak.

Looking over his now shining armor, Valerius nodded. "Excellent job," he told the skeleton.

Once done, the undead walked away to its other chores.

Valerius boldly stepped up to the front door of the castle. "Come along, my good cohorts. We aren't going to get anything accomplished by standing here."

Forming a fist, he prepared to knock on the door. With a curse, Shadow grabbed hold of the man's wrist. "What are you doing?" Shadow asked.

"I'm going to knock on the door and demand this villain give himself up and mend his evil ways. He will have to give up his hold on this helpless princess and allow her to return to her family safe and whole."

Pixel narrowed her eyes at the fighter. "Have you ever done this before?" she demanded.

"No," he answered honestly. His cheeks turned red. "My wife wouldn't approve of me rescuing another woman." He pulled his wrist free of Shadow's grip and banged on the door.

The heavy oak door opened with an ominous creak to a black foyer. With a shrug, Valerius led the heroes into the black void. In the middle of the room, a ghostly image of the man depicted on the fountain appeared.

"Welcome to the castle of Gozleckia," he announced with a smile. The expression widened on his noble face, as he raised his hand and cast a spell, "It will be your grave."

Chapter 5

Uttering a curse, Roland fell forward off balance. Sensing he was in a different place, he raised up in a crouch and twitched his nose. His delicate little hands were held out in front of him, as he sniffed the air.

The room was lit by dim candlelight. Twitching his mouth into a sneer, he found the wooden paneling and floor free of all dirt and vermin. The smell of wood oil and freshly mopped floors assaulted his senses. He cursed. He much preferred the comforts of home with the stench of rotting garbage and buzzing pests. Besides, he needed a good snack. When faced with such a puzzling situation, he did what he normally did. He flopped back on his butt. Positioning himself in a way that no human could possibly do, he scratched the back of his ear with his foot.

An idea lit the dark corridors of his musty brain. He got up and turned around. He found a vast table set before him with every nameable kind of food upon it and laid out in the most succulent splendor. At the far end of the table was a ghostly apparition. Like their host, this ghost wore fine, aristocratic clothes. Unlike that specter, he was a round fellow.

With all the finery around him, one would have thought this jovial being to be some sort of a king before a feast, except for the skull ornaments he wore on his head and waist. Before him on the table was a plate of meats and desserts.

Upon closer inspection, Roland saw where all the vermin had gone. The plate was crawling with every known pestilence, bugs of all description and other unsavory critters. This did not seem to bother the diner any, as he stuffed his mouth with his bare hands with no regard for the utensils at his elbows or the vermin in his food.

Roland moved forward to the table. The otherworldly nature of the occupant and the crawling things did little to bother him. He was bred and born in the back alleys of Shady Valley. To tell the truth, he did his fair share of breeding in the same alleys. He had seen worse.

He poked at the nearest bowl of pudding. Several beetles scurried out of it. Roland's eyes widened as did his smile.

"It's got the crunchy bits!" he exclaimed.

The ghost watched him with a smile on his fat face. Something happened, and the ghost's eyes crossed. His jaws swelled to twice their size. Once capacity was reached, the ghost opened his mouth and let loose a tremendous belch.

Roland jumped up on the table. Picking off a couple of roaches from the pig, he sat astride the roasted animal. "That was good one, my lord," he told him.

"Thank you." The ghost gave him a great toothy grin. "I am the dread necromancer known as the Pestilence."

Roland sat back and puffed out his chest proudly. "I've been called that often!" he told him.

"I am here to squash your soul from your body for my unholy master. Your lifeless body will lie here and be feasted upon by my pets."

Roland pulled a hunk of pork out of his seat and stuffed it in his mouth. Swallowing down most of it, he replied, "I've heard worse from my wife. She offered to pull my brains out my nose to pay off the zombie patrol. Didn't work, mind you. She didn't find any, but she did find a big wad of snot."

The ghost cocked an eyebrow that just crawled away into his hair. "You have no fear of my undead splendor?"

"Nah. You're just a ghost," Roland remarked, as he scooped up some of the oozing relish at his feet. His beady eyes lit up at the taste. "This is really good, you know!" he exclaimed.

The ghost's expression softened. "Yes, it is! Quite a meal after 1500 years of nothing. I told my master that he had better make this a good one, if he wanted me to do his dirty work."

Leaning back on the pig, Roland looked around at all the fine foods. "I'd say. Quite a feast indeed!"

"Try some of the pate."

I think I will at that!" replied Roland, as he dipped his hand into the creamy stuff. "Ever had fish and chip from a greasy street vendor?" he asked. "Especially one crawling with all sorts of lice?"

"No. Tell me more!" the Pestilence encouraged.

And, so the conversation and the feast went on until Roland finally rolled off the table. He landed on the floor on his back. His hand rested on his swollen belly, and sonorous snores ripped from his throat.

Rubbing his spectral full belly with one hand, the ghostly wizard snapped the fingers of the other hand. Two decaying, worm eaten zombies appeared. The Pestilence casually pulled a long worm from his mindless slave. The worm squirmed and caught hold of the ghostly wrist. There it curled itself around like a bracelet.

"Take away the trash," he ordered the undead minions.

Without a word, one zombie took up Roland's ankles and the other his wrists. They carried him away.

The Pestilence sat back in his chair and pulled the worm from his wrist. "Pity. He was a nice enough of a fellow. I hate to dispose of him, but a job is a job." With that, he dropped the worm in his mouth.

Chapter 6

Pixel found herself in a room with racks and racks of fancy clothes and jewelry. Opening her eyes wide, she knew exactly what to do. Looking around, she made sure no one saw her. If no one knew she did it, then she didn't do it. She stuffed as much of the jewelry into her pouches as she could. With a word of magic she had learned from her pixie family, the load reduced its size into a more portable bundle and one more easily concealed.

Running her hands along the fine clothes, she stopped at one exquisite blue gown. Pulling it down, she held it in front of herself. Looking down, at the dress, she shook her head. The feel of the silken fabric against her body did not give her the full advantage of her appearance. Moving through the maze of clothes, she found a mirror. Smiling, she moved in front of it and admired what she saw there. With a girlish giggle, she knew her glamor. She looked the part of an elven princess, instead of a half breed outcast.

Finding a necklace of blue gems, she put it around her neck, then she added a tiara with the same kind of gem. Yes, indeed. She made a truly striking figure of a woman. What man could resist her charms? Besides, these gems would fetch a good price.

A pair of earrings floated below each of her ears. "These would make the final touches. Aquamarine is definitely your color. It matches your eyes perfectly. Now, we must get you out of those drab clothes. I can help you there."

With a cry, she dropped the dress like it was a ravenous raccoon and jumped atop a chair. The bow was instantly in her hands, and an arrow was notched. The missile was aimed at a tall, regal, spectral figure of a man, holding the earrings. His hair was slicked back, and he sported a finely curled mustache and a little pointed beard at the very edge of his chin. He may have been attractive in his living days, but something sinister lurked around his being. A sheepish smile crossed his thin lips.

Seeing her disapproval, he dropped the ear accessories and held up his hands. A wider smile crossed his serpentine lips, showing off his longer than normal canines. His dead eyes sparkled as he looked over her petite, elvish form. A hint of a smirk crossed those lips, as his eyes lingered on her shapely thighs so well outlined by her hose.

Pixel, recognizing that look, strengthened her pose. She pulled back on the arrow with the string taunt. The ghost merely laughed.

"I am beyond the effects of your mortal weapons. Besides, what kind of a sportsmanship is it to shoot a man, who appreciates your fine assets?"

The arrow flew. It passed through his immaterial face and thunked into the wall behind him.

"Tsk, tsk! What ill manners!" he complained. Shaking his head, he made an elaborate bow to her. "I forget mine as well. Introductions are in order. I am called the Death Master by my peers."

She snorted. "You didn't master death too well by the look of it," she remarked.

"Well, we all make mistakes, and my master was more than happy to point out that flaw as well. So, tell me your name, my sweet, and introductions will be complete."

"I know better than let a necromancer know my name. Your kind practice all manner of devious things with the name. I've been with the goof ball wizard too long not to know a few things."

"It doesn't matter, anyway." With a wave of his hand, the ghost revealed several well-dressed skeletons, carrying some of the finest clothes, made from silks, satin, and velvet. "No matter your name, your beauty is the same, and beauty such as yours should be wrapped in the finest of materials," he announced. A smile lifted his lips into that familiar leer. "Of course, I do fancy you without."

The nearest skeleton reached out for her. With a hard hit from her bow, she knocked it out of her way. She danced over the back of the chair into the sea of clothes. Disappearing under the racks, she made her way through the twists and turns of this labyrinth. After some time, she emerged into the open air once again. She stood up and looked around to get her bearings.

The racks of clothes around her disappeared and were replaced by mirrors. Her reflection appeared in the infinite corridors of the reflection's reflection. An infinite rose appeared before her. She turned around until her eyes met with the ghosts. She took a step backwards and stumbled into one of the mirrors

"For one as beautiful and delicate as you, there is no comparison. This poor rose pales in comparison."

Not exactly being the damsel in distress, she threw a kick to the ghost's knees. Dropping the rose, her courting pursuer did not move to avoid the impact. Her foot went through his immaterial body. Thrown off balance, she hopped around on one foot. The Death Master laughed and grabbed her ankle.

"You know the ankle is the sexiest part of the female anatomy," he purred to her.

"You filthy lech!" she growled and struggled to free herself.

"Just because I am dead, doesn't mean I can't appreciate the aesthetics of young flesh."

Laughing, he pulled her leg up higher. Being born of two incredibly limber races, she was able to twist herself around and bite her captor in the butt. Letting out a delighted yelp, he released her.

"Ooo! A feisty one!" he exclaimed, as he rubbed his rear end. A grin crossed his face. "I like them feisty!"

He grabbed for her, but she jumped at one of the mirrors. The prop fell over and revealed the room of clothes again. She dove back into the maze. At the first rack, she made a turn. The clothes on either side of her brushed against her shoulders and neck. Sweat beaded on her brow and around her neck, and she gasped for air. Relentlessly, the racks of clothes continued on, as if they would close in upon her.

With a deep breath, as if diving under water, she ducked under the nearest rack and closed her eyes. Exhaustion threatened to overtake her. But after a few moments rest, she braced herself and continued. She would never get out of this maze if she gave up.

Crawling on the floor, she came to an opening and emerged into another row of material. After several minutes of twists and turns in the suffocating darkness and close quarters, she saw a light. Hope flared. It would be enough to be away from this enclosing burial. She ran towards the opening heedless of the dangers.

Breaking free into the open once again, she found herself in the ghost's arms, and she was none too pleased where his hands landed on her anatomy.

"Oh, love. We were just meant to be," he mused as he took her shoulders and held her at arm's length.

Being pinned by his strength, she did the only option she had left to her. She spat in his eyes.

Laughing, he only blinked away the saliva. He pulled her into his face. "What a spitfire! You awaken parts of me that I no longer thought worked!"

Pulling her in even closer, he gave her a deep kiss. Struggle as she might, she could not break free. He sucked her breath out. As consciousness left her, she wished she still had that dagger or sharp shoes to stab her opponent. Her petite body soon crumpled into his ghostly arms.

With a wave of his hand, one of the well-dressed skeletons picked up her unconscious body. "Take her to the dungeon," he ordered, as he smoothed down his ruffled clothes. "Ah, but alas, poor lass. She knows not what she is missing out on." He laid a rose on her chest.

If the skeletons had been sentient, they would have fallen on the floor in fierce laughter. But they were merely puppets, controlled by this dead necromancer's power. So, they remained silent, as they carried out their orders.

Chapter 7

Valerius found himself in an arena. Immediately, he drew his sword and spread his feet. The hairs on the back of his neck stood up in attention, and the prickles of dark magic bit at his back and shoulders like fleas on a dog. Evil was here, but as he squinted his eyes and looked around, he knew it was just not visible yet.

At first the stands were empty, but with a ripple and a gust of coldness, they became populated. The air shimmered. Skeletons and zombies appeared scattered throughout the stands. The air shifted again, and less corporeal beings, like formless ghosts and wraiths, peppered among their more solid brethren, like a chess board in black and white. Valerius' stance did not waver.

The air on the battlefield swirled with cold and dust, and several armored skeletons approached him with drawn swords and spears. Their fleshless jaws jabbered in silent accusations. Flexing his muscles under his armor, Valerius raised his sword. With a prayer to Eleysius, the god of the righteous, he made an expert strike to all his mindless attackers in one fluid movement. The skeletons fell into a pile of inanimate bones. The undead audience made negative noises of boos and hisses.

"Hmm," remarked a deep voice of a man. A pile of bones rattled, and the ghostly form of a hulking man in a simple loin cloth appeared. Thick muscles of a well-trained fighter rippled across his body. He flexed his biceps in a rhythmic fashion, then the triceps. Turning around, he flexed his deltoids and his well-formed, mostly exposed, gluteus maximus. The ghost turned around to face his opponent. Small eyes glared out from under a heavy brow, and his undercut jaw suggested that he had more than his fair share of ogre in his blood.

"I am the fantastic, magnificent necromancer known as the Corpse Ripper," he announced, as he twirled around like a ballerina. Choosing a zombie from the audience, the ghost raised his hand. The undead floated to the necromancer and fell on the ground before hm. With a show of flexing muscles, the Corpse Ripper picked up the body and held it over his head. With a flick of his finger, the audience cheered. Giving a good grunt, he ripped the zombie in two. More cheers. Raising his hands, the ghost made a round of bows. The separate pieces of the zombie crawled off in opposite directions.

Finally, after the show, the ghost turned to his opponent and gave a lopsided smile. "Shall we see how your corpse rips?"

"Indeed we shall, you foul, undead monster! With the aid of Eleysius, I shall send your unclean spirit back to Hell, where it belongs!"

"Just try it, boy," the Corpse Ripper challenged, as he barreled forward.

Jumping out of the way of the onslaught, Valerius stumbled, but quickly caught his balance. Believing firmly in the laws of fair play, he threw the sword aside. The Corpse ripper turned around to make a second swipe. With a laugh, Valerius crouched down into a wrestler's pose with his full armor still on.

The battle was embarrassingly short. The Corpse Ripper ran at him with full force. A resounding thud filled the arena as the two impacted. The solid force of the ghost bowled Valerius over on his back. Being a man of some considerable strength, Valerius held onto his opponent. Laughing, the ghost became immaterial and floated out of his grip.

"No fair!" the knight complained.

"I never said I played by the rules," the ghost remarked with a wink. "After all, I am a dead evil necromancer."

Valerius flared like a turtle on his back. His armor weighing a goodly amount made it impossible for him to pull himself back up. "A hand here, if you please," Valerius requested.

With a laugh, the Corpse Ripper walked over to Valerius and looked down on him. The ghost bonked him on the head. The force of the blow knocked Valerius out cold. The ghost lifted the heavy armored man up over his head, and the cheers of the undead audience filled the arena.

Throwing Valerius over his shoulder, the Corpse Ripper headed for the dungeon. "What a disappointment! I was hoping to show off my signature Skull Crusher move," he complained.

With a wave of his hand, the defeated skeletal warriors rose and followed him.

Chapter 8

Shadow found himself in a hallway, surrounded by doors with various signs on them. One read, "kitchen", then "pantry", "laundry", "laboratory", then "lavatory". Shadow took a visit to this last one before continuing onward. It had been a long journey. After being refreshed, he continued his exploration. He seriously doubted that he would find the door marked "Tower Prison with Princess", but he had nothing else left to do but continue walking. He came upon an intersecting corridor with more doors on either side. Stroking his chin, he looked down the left one, then down the right one.

At a loss as to which to choose, he dug through his clothes to find his money pouch. To his relief, it was still there. Opening it, he poured the contents into his hand. Just as at the tavern, there was nothing of use in it. Throwing the purse on the floor, he sat there in a dejected meditation.

A scream of bloody terror awoke him from his self-pity. Scrambling to his feet, he ran down the corridor from which it came. A second scream confirmed the proper door. With his hand on the handle, he paused to read the sign. It read, "Torture Chamber. Do Not Disturb!" Shadow pulled back and scratched his head. The third desperate scream made up his mind. Kicking the door open wide, he entered into the unknown.

Shadow found himself in a dimly lit chamber with several sparkling chains and hooks hanging down the walls. A wooden bed with pristine shackles for wrists and ankles and perfect crank wheels held the center of the room. Cages, barely big enough to hold an average sized human hung from the ceiling. They also shined, as if they were freshly brought here from the blacksmith. Although all evidence pointed to what the sign had announced, there was no blood, dirt, or remains anywhere. The air was fresh and clean. No scent of blood or decay tainted the air. In fact, there was a vague scent of perfume. Vermin also seemed to be oddly absent. Usually, such scenes had a scurrying rat or two gnawing bones.

The wizard's puzzlement was short lived and replaced with a new sensation. A delicate, pale woman with flowing raven black hair stood in front of him. Her piercing sapphire eyes peered at him from a red, leather mask that covered on the upper half of her face. Blood red lips frowned, and he stood back to notice the rest of her outfit. She wore knee-high boots and elbow-length gloves of the same red color. The rest of her outfit consisted of strips of leather that covered only the strategic spots. In her hands, she held a bullwhip.

Shadow's eyes grew wide, and he swallowed hard. "What in the seven hells is this?"

"Oh!" the woman cried out in surprise. With a snap of her fingers, her whole outfit and demeanor changed. She was now wearing a flowing yellow gown complete with a conical hat. A snatch of yellow veil flowed down around her delicate form like a halo. Clutching her hands together, she looked up at him with pleading eyes.

"Please, dear sir. Save me from the horrible lich before he can complete his terrible plans for me," she begged in a beautiful, musical voice.

"Marissa?" called a soft, refined voice. "May I take these chains off now?" A skeleton entered the room. Unlike the other undead of this variety, he was naked except for the broken chains and shackles around his wrists and ankles.

Shadow took a step backwards and surveyed the scene before him. This skeleton stood better than a foot shorter than him, but the blue flame eyes in the empty eye sockets told him that this was a sentient undead. This had to be the undead wizard they had set out to challenge, and the woman had to be his captive. The lessons he had received in wizardry had said that this lich would be no easy target. Yet somehow, Shadow always thought that such beings would tower over him.

The lich made visual contact with him and jumped noticeably. With a movement of his boney left hand, he made fine black robes appear over his frame. The chains clattered to the ground, as the lich floated upwards to make himself taller than Shadow.

"Who are you, who dares invade my castle?" he demanded.

"Uh . . ." answered Shadow.

When faced with overwhelming odds, Shadow did what he usually did. He only had come to rescue the princess. So, he grabbed her up and threw her over his shoulder. He made a run for it. The door was only a few feet away, and the lich had not blasted him yet. He might just make it. He felt a sudden jab of a dagger in his back.

Dropping his burden, he stopped in his tracks. He dug the blade out of his back. Looking at the weapon in his hand, he felt sick, and the room spun around. A black ichor mixed with his own blood dripped off the blade. The burn of the poison spread outward from his wound. Before he could utter the proper curse, he crumpled to the ground.

The princess pulled herself up and took the dagger from his nerveless fingers. The lich floated to her and looked down at the fallen victim. His jaw shifted slightly, and he shook his head.

"You could have left something for me to do," he complained.

"But this was so much more fun! Did you see that expression on his face when he realized what I had done?" she asked as she licked the blood from her blade.

"Are you not afraid of poisoning yourself with your own craft?" he asked.

"All good poisoners acquire an immunity to their own tools," she replied, as she tapped her forefinger on the bone bridge of his nose.

Shaking his head, he took her hand. She in turn took up Shadow's limp wrist. The lich raised his free left hand and made several signs. The three of them disappeared.

Chapter 9

To his surprise, Shadow did not wake up in Hell or any other World of the Dead he had heard of. Instead, he woke up in what appeared to be a clean, well-kept dungeon with a comfortable straw mattress under his back and no interesting graffiti on the wall. No scent of stale urine or other excrement assaulted his sense of smell. In fact, there was a soft scent of lavender.

Turning over, he saw a tray of feasible food, steak and potatoes. Sitting up, he felt the rumble in his stomach. The meal even smelled good. It was not what he was used to, and he had been in a good many prisons. Poking his meal, he noticed that it seemed well cooked and did not bite back like Pixel's cooking.

It seemed to be a harmless enough dish of meat and potatoes. Having not eaten for some time and all traces of the poison seemed removed from his system, he took up the tray without any more hesitation and wolfed it down.

"Once you're done, can I have the leftovers?" Roland asked.

Swallowing down the last sizeable bite, Shadow looked around the prison. His companions were there, and they seemed safe and whole. How strange that a lich would not kill or mangle any of them. Even stranger, none of them seemed to be undead.

"Thanks to you, we're all stuck in this dungeon!" complained Pixel.

"How do you figure?" Shadow shot back.

"It was your idea to go on this stupid quest in the first place! I just wanted to stake out and rob a good mansion. No. We had to do something heroic and legitimate this time!" Pixel voiced her explanation.

"But the food is really good here," Roland added, as he took Shadow's plate and licked at the leftover gravy.

"Yes. We're treated well for prisoners, especially prisoners of such a villain," Valerius told him. Wearing a simple tunic and hose, the knight sat on a bed side and was polishing his armor. With a nod, he admired his work. "A very pleasant young man came in with the meals and performed healing spells on you. I would say that was some poison used on you. Your body was all purple and jerking in some nasty spasms."

"Yeah, well, I found the princess. I don't think she wanted rescuing," he replied, as he scratched his head. "She might be under some kind of wicked spell from that lich!"

A flash of light filled the cell, and a puff of black smoke rolled around the floor and outside the bars of the cell. In the midst of the smoke appeared a black figure. A hood hung over his face and obscured his features, but the fleshless lower jaw was visible. The fierce blue flame burned deep within the darkness of the hood. His arms, covered in heavy black sleeves, were crossed. The bare bone fingers grasped at his elbows.

Having seen more impressive entrances, Roland continued to lick the plate. Besides, this was what Valerius was here to defend him against. Secretly, he smiled to himself. It was good to be such a lowly creature and below the contempt of the powerful.

"What do you want with us?" Valerius demanded.

With a forced gruffness in his voice, the lich answered him. "You have trespassed upon my home. I will see you dead, then I will resurrect your carcasses, worm eaten and full of maggots, to fight alongside my undead army. I will see this world festering at my feet."

"If you can find your feet," remarked Pixel.

The bone forefinger of his left hand pointed at the small woman. "You! Shut up!"

Valerius looked at the lich and furrowed his brow. "I know you, don't I?"

"Foolish mortal! If we had met, you would be dead and enslaved to my will!" growled the lich.

Roland suddenly cried out. The group turned their attention to the little man. A black cat sat on his plate. Roland jumped up and disappeared out of his clothes. A rat ran out the pile and through the bars of the cell easily.

The lich pulled back and stumbled. He fell into the dissipating smoke. An otherworldly scream filled the air, as the rat scrambled around. Confused by the commotion, the rodent ran up the lich's robes.

"Get it off me!" the lich cried out, as he struggled and kicked.

Four living people of various races came out of the shadows. They ran to the fallen undead wizard's aid. Once the lich calmed, a young man with long brown hair, streaked with gray, went to the cell. Although the hair was combed to cover the left side of his face, his exposed green eye was opened wide.

"Pepper! What are you doing in there?" he cried out, as he opened the cell door.

At the sound of his name, the cat looked up a moment, then returned his attention to the commotion. Like any other house cat, as soon as the door was opened, he left the plate behind and ran over to where the action was. A movement caught his feline eyes. Raising his hind quarters, he waggled them, paused, and bounded forward. The rat ran out of the undead wizard's clothes and fled down the hallway. The cat followed in pursuit.

The prisoners walked out into the hallway, since the door had been left opened. Shadow recognized the princess among the people around the lich. She was now dressed in a simpler dress, and she wrapped her arms around the undead wizard, who hid his face in her neck and hair. Stroking his head and back, she spoke soothing words to him.

The remaining two people in the group were the wizard and his apprentice from the tavern. Since neither Shadow or Pixel had seen them, they did not recognize them. Valerius, on the other hand, gave the two a salute of greeting. Standing up straight, the knight crossed his arms and glared at the lich.

"Malhavoc, what are you doing?" Valerius demanded. "It has been five years since I have seen you!"

The lich pried himself out of the woman's embrace and sat up in a more respectable way. Throwing back his hood, he met the warrior's gaze. "It is my honeymoon. You would know this if you showed up at my wedding," he complained. "Marissa and I set up this trap to do in some of you do-gooders."

"It was fun!" Marissa added.

"And?" Valerius prodded.

Turning his skull to look away from him, Malhavoc answered him. "Nikodemus will not allow me to kill any of you. So, do not get all righteous on me. No one is hurt. Galen, my recent addition as my apprentice, has been studying under me for the last two years. He has turned out to be a good healer, despite my efforts otherwise. He has been taking care of those who fall in battle. I keep you trespassers for a couple of days and do what I can to terrorize you, then I send you off to somewhere far away from me."

Marissa wrapped her arms around Malhavoc's middle and squeezed into the hallow under his rib cage. The lich squirmed as she touched his hidden pelvic bone. Casually, he moved her hands up to his chest. She cuddled her face into his neck. "You have been so romantic when you get rid of them, too!"

"And it has been a learning experience, too," Malhavoc muttered.

Shadow and Pixel looked to each other in confusion. "What kind of a lich is afraid of rats?" Shadow demanded.

"You!" Malhavoc growled, pointing his bone finger at him. "Shut up! You become a lich while being eaten alive by rats and tell me that it does not have an adverse effect on you."

"Liches don't fall in love with pretty girls!" Shadow added.

"And the other way around," Pixel put in as well.

"They are an exceptional couple," Nikodemus remarked. "I told Mal that I could use someone to clean up Gozleckia after we defeated the evil here. So, he got his ghost friends . . ."

"Slaves . . ." muttered Malhavoc.

". . . friends to raise all the discarded bodies around here to do the job. Mal was even able to bring back the dread necromancer The

Eternal Darkness as a ghost under his control."

"So, there's no princess?" complained Shadow.

"No treasure," complained Pixel.

"Marissa is a princess," Valerius told them. "She's my half-sister. Her mother is the elven queen of Greenwood. My father got around."

"I say," Malhavoc remarked, as he pulled himself to his feet and dusted down his robes. Looking up, he met Valerius's gaze. "And what are you doing rescuing a princess? What would Judel say?"

"What Judel doesn't know, won't hurt her," Valerius replied with a blush. "After all, it's not like I expect any kind of reward from a princess. Judel is enough of a woman for me!"

"Yeah, well," Malhavoc remarked. "You get that rat out of here, and we both will forget about this whole situation."

"What about us?" Shadow complained.

"You cannot have the princess! She is mine!" Malhavoc cried out. Marissa wrapped her arms around him again and gave him a deep kiss. The undead wizard flared out his arms at first, then he relaxed. He pushed her off. "Not now, woman!"

"Later then," she whispered, as she ran her fingers down his breast bone. Malhavoc shuffled his feet uncomfortably.

Shadow and Pixel looked at each other. "How?" queried Shadow.

"Do not ask!" the lich shot back, as he watched Marissa dance away. "I am a talented and well accomplished necromancer, after all." Turning his skull to look at the couple before him, he straightened his shoulders. "What would you have me do?"

"I want treasure," Pixel demanded simply. "I don't work for free."

"Woman, any treasure you can wrest away from my associates is yours. I have no need for it, and Marissa is happy with the money her mother sends her and the wages she earns from the apothecary in town."

"I need a good wizard master," Shadow told him hopefully.

"And you would get this from rescuing a princess?" the lich

asked.

"Well, no, but you can't provide me with what I wanted from that venture. I wouldn't want it from you anyway! I'm not of that persuasion."

Malhavoc growled a vile Kruskusian curse. "You are not gaining any winning points for your request."

"Ah, come on, Mal," Nikodemus encouraged. "Make the boy your apprentice. It could be fun."

The flames burned fiercer in the lich's eye sockets. "What do I look like? The school for messed up wizards? You take him on. Tallon is ready to graduate from your schooling."

"Oh, hush!" Nikodemus told him. "You know you enjoy showing off what you know."

Turning to Shadow, the lich looked him up and down. Pausing, he observed the young man's strange eyes. Holding out his hand for Shadow's hand, he wanted to assess the power within him. Shadow pulled away. Cocking his head, the lich returned his hands to his sleeves.

"You do understand what I am, and you fear. Excellent," he remarked. He hooked his thumb at Nikodemus, Tallon, and Galen. "They have no clue about the horrors of the undead. Galen is the worst of the lot. He truly thinks that I am a nice person! It will be good to have an apprentice with some sense." With a movement of his left hand, he cast a spell on Shadow. Malhavoc cocked his head and nodded. "Yes. You have some tainted dark magic. I will take you on. It may prove rewarding to me. You may be able to teach Galen something while you are at it."

"You mean it!" Shadow exclaimed. "This is great! You aren't about to get eaten by anything like my last master did! You don't look that appetizing." Losing all trepidations, the young man threw his arms around the undead wizard. "Thank you so much!"

Pushing the clinging man off of him, Malhavoc grumbled, "How do I get myself into such messes?"

IT JUST DRIVES ME CRAZY
by Gary Reed

Author Note: My novel *A Fatal Cell Phone Video*, originally published as *Explicit Bias*, concerns the murder of Ann Lindsey Medawar, the wife of a rakishly handsome surgeon, Rafiq A. Medawar, M.D. When the police find Ann's body in a park overlooking the Ohio River, they discover on her cell phone a video of her husband and a nurse going into a sleazy inn.

The Prosecutor, Richard Warren, assumes that Dr. Medawar and the nurse were having an affair, his wife confronted him, and he killed her. Warren is running for higher office on an anti-immigration and anti-Muslim platform. When he is informed, incorrectly, that Dr. Medawar is a Syrian immigrant, he makes the prosecution a prop to his campaign.

Dr. Medawar tells his attorney that the nurse and Ann persuaded him to go the inn to check on the sick children of an undocumented woman. Ann was taking a course on documentary making and made the video of him and the nurse entering the inn for use in the class project, a documentary about the plight of the undocumented. His version of events is undercut by the fact that the police did not find an undocumented woman with children at the inn, and the inn's manager denies that anyone fitting that description stayed at the inn.

The material below follows two minor, but important characters, Emily Goessel and her attorney, Weary Dunston, who seemingly hold the key to the case. This story includes material taken from the novel and one additional section. *G.R.*

1.

Driving a red, late-model Mercedes 350 sedan, Emily Goessel, forty, was hurrying through Clifton on her way to her kids' school. She had just learned from the school nurse that her daughter, Brittany, had the measles. The nurse had demanded someone pick up Brittany as soon as possible –implying that Brittany was putting other kids at risk. Goessel didn't understand the fuss. When she was a kid, everyone got the measles. It was no big deal.

She –not her husband– had picked up their son, Dylan, a week and a half ago, when he too came down the measles. She –not her husband– had to put up with the nurse and school principal demanding to know if her kids had been vaccinated. And have them end up autistic? Not a chance. And she –not her husband– had to deflect their questions about how she had procured certifications that their kids had been vaccinated, when they hadn't been.

She felt it was her husband's turn to do the school run and put up with the vaccination Nazis. But her husband refused, claiming he had clients in from out-of-town and couldn't possibly leave. Why was his job always more important than hers? She had meetings too. Granted, he made several times what she did and they couldn't afford him getting fired, but they were his kids too. He needed to act like a father once in a while.

Caught up in her own thoughts, Goessel did not notice the police cruiser following her with its light flashing. It was only when the policeman briefly turned on the cruiser's siren that she realized she was speeding and about to get a ticket.

She turned down the aptly-named Travelers Lane, three blocks of fast food restaurants and what-have-you, and began looking for a place to pull over. None of the fast food restaurant parking lots on either side of the street seemed suitable. Just her luck, someone she knew would see the whole humiliating thing.

When the cop turned his siren on again, she cursed and abruptly pulled into the next parking lot. After she did, she realized she had pulled into the parking lot of the Sleep Cheap Inn. Only the worst possible place on the whole street.

When she parked her car, the police cruiser turned its siren off. Before searching her glove department for her registration papers, Goessel glanced back at the police car and its occupant. The cop, she thought, looked like he was twenty-something. It was beyond annoying that some kid was about to give her a ticket and a lecture on speeding.

It was her worthless, no-good, too-busy-for-his-family husband's fault. If he had picked up Brittany, she wouldn't be the one getting the ticket.

2.

Assigned to patrol duty in the city's Fifth District, Cincinnati Police Department officer Eleanor Billington was making her way down McMillan Street when she saw the Cincinnati police cruiser turn into Travelers Lane with its siren on. She recognized the patrolman. He was Peter Browne. Tall, good-looking, handsome-in-his-uniform, no-wedding-band Peter Browne.

Billington flipped on her own siren and followed Browne's cruiser down the side street. She pulled into the parking lot of the "hot sheets" inn and parked alongside Browne's black and white.

Billington was almost 30, which likely made her a couple years older than Browne. That might or might not rule out a long-term relationship, but since she had first met Browne, she had been intrigued by him. For the moment, however, she was just wondering if he would be available for lunch. She turned her siren off and got out of her vehicle. Browne, she could see, was noting the license plate number of the red Mercedes and going through the usual protocols.

Billington gave Browne a big, flirtatious grin. "Thought you might need some backup," she greeted him. "She's looks pretty dangerous to me."

"I like my women dangerous," Browne responded.

3.

Emily Goessel saw the two officers chatting, and taking their time about it. She fumed as she watched the lady cop flirt with the patrolman. She was frustrated that there was nothing she could do about it – until it occurred to her that there was something she could do.

She pulled her cell phone from her purse, rolled down the car window, and ostentatiously began videoing the two officers. She knew her video wasn't going to be as sensational as all those videos of white police officers beating some black man while he lays on the street or sidewalk trying to cover his head. But, she told herself, that wasn't the point.

She figured once the cops saw her making a video of them chatting and flirting, they would hurry up and get this over with. Who knew, she thought, warming to the topic, rather than have me email the video to their superiors or post it on the internet, maybe they will let me off with a warning? Maybe, she told herself, as the two cops continued their conversation, they won't want the world to know that a mother was delayed from picking up her sick child while they leisurely shot the breeze.

The officers didn't notice.

Goessel tried to hold her cell phone steady, but it wasn't as easy as it sounded.

And then, just because it was one of those days when nothing goes right, some jerks walked between her car and the police cars, inserting themselves into the video she was trying to make. They were two tough-looking Mexican men, a young Mexican woman, and her two small kids. Goessel had heard all sorts of rumors about the inn, from it being a transit point for drugs to being a favorite waystation for illegals. These people just seemed to confirm all the rumors she had heard.

Perfect, Goessel thought. Everybody knows this inn is nothing but trouble, and these two cops are so busy talking, a bunch of illegals go walking right by, and they don't even notice.

She followed the Mexicans with her cell phone camera as they crowded into a worn-out, blue Honda and drove off. She turned her camera back in the direction of the police officers, but their conversation was ending.

As the young patrolman approached her car, Goessel kept her video running. She wanted to be sure the cop understood that she was not happy –and had him on video flirting with the female cop.

"Sorry for the delay, Ma'am," the young patrolman said.

That was his way, Goessel supposed, of letting her know he could see what she was doing the cell phone. "My child is sick," she announced, reaching for the moral high ground. "The school called and said my daughter is very sick. They asked me to come and get her as soon as possible."

"I'm sorry to hear that, Ma'am, but—"

"My child is sick and crying and begging for her mother," Goessel asserted with no more exaggeration than she thought was her right, "and I'm sitting here while you have a gabfest with your cop friend. I want—"

"Ma'am," the young cop interrupted, "you were going well over the speed limit. Those speed limits are set to keep people safe. It wouldn't help your daughter if you had an accident and were seriously hurt or killed. Or if you injured or killed some other kid's mother."

"Oh for chrissake's, no one had an accident, and no one's been injured or killed. I want you to know that—"

"Ma'am," the patrolman interrupted again. "I need to see your license, registration and proof of insurance."

"I've been sitting here with them in my hand for five minutes,"

Goessel fired back, even though the actual time was not half that. It galled her no end that the patrolman wanted to see her papers, but ignored the illegals who walked right by him.

She surrendered the papers to the patrolman. "I want you to know," she continued, "that I'm going to make sure your superiors see my video of you and that woman officer taking your good time while my daughter is sick, begging for her mother."

"You do what you have to do, Ma'am," Browne responded. "Let's just get this done as quickly as we can, so you can get your daughter. I'm going to be right back."

Five minutes later, Goessel had her ticket and was on her way – mentally preparing for the day's next battle.

Just one word from the school nurse busybody about vaccinations, she told herself, and she's going to wish she had minded her own business.

4.

After her husband pointed out that her speeding ticket was her third moving violation in less than a year, Goessel was beside herself. She could not have her license suspended. If she had to, she would attend those awful classes, but really, she didn't see why she should even have to do that. She had a friend who had to go to those classes, and she said they had been dreadful. Most of the people in those classes were losers. Her friend said it was worse than shopping at Walmart. She, Goessel insisted, had nothing in common with *those* people.

Tired of listening to his wife grouse about why her traffic tickets were his fault, Larry Goessel contacted the law firm his company used. It was one of the city's top firms, with offices in the downtown business district. He spoke with the corporate lawyer with whom he usually worked and asked her if there was anything the firm could do to help his wife.

She in turn contacted the head of the firm's litigation section, Hayden Lassiter Barrington, V, whom everyone called Quint, to see how the firm handled such requests. She assumed the firm would send a litigation associate to traffic court with the client. But Quint had no desire to have the firm's young lawyers pulled off profitable matters to deal with a client's traffic ticket. He knew from bitter experience the client would be unhappy with the result, and the firm would end up writing off most of the time involved. Besides, traffic court was an awful place, and he did want not his talented young litigators wasting their time there.

After making a call to be sure the pompous old pettifogger was still practicing and would take the case, Quint referred Emily Goessel to Weary Dunston, the "dean" of the traffic court bar. He assured Goessel that Dunston routinely represented the firm's clients in such matters, and that there was no one who knew the traffic court personnel better. He would also be much less expensive.

5.

Emily Goessel was somewhat mollified that she would be represented by the dean of the traffic court —a real veteran who knew his way around that madhouse— until she met the old goat and realized having to deal with him would be yet another humiliation. His suit was older than her kids! And to add insult to injury, Dunston insisted on payment in advance, like she was one of his usual deadbeat clients.

Goessel explained to Dunston the extenuating circumstances surrounding her speeding ticket—the call from the school that her daughter was sick with a potentially fatal illness.

Dunston was certain that the court, which heard such excuses all day long, would not be impressed. The court would want to know one thing: Was she driving over the speed limit?

Goessel could only imagine what traffic court judges might have to put up with, but she thought the phlegmy old litigator was too dismissive of her special circumstances. She was not the sort of riff-raff the traffic court judges usually had to deal with. Surely, the fact that she was not one of those people would matter for something.

Dunston was unconvinced.

Everything about this was unfair, Goessel complained, launching into her explanation about how, when the cop turned his siren on, she made the mistake of pulling into the parking lot of that fleabag inn –the one where Ace Lindsey's daughter caught her husband having a fling with that Filipino nurse. And then the young traffic cop, who was probably still in his twenties, had made her sit there while he flirted with some lady cop. Her daughter was sick, but that came first?

She insisted Dunston watch the video on her cell phone. As he did, she pointed out the injustice that neither cop had shown the least interest in the Mexicans, who were probably illegals here for the free benefits, but she had to show her identification? Really? Whose country was it?

Dunston grunted when the video finished and returned the cell phone without saying more.

Upset that the old geezer did not seem sufficiently stirred to indignation, Goessel redoubled her efforts. "You know," she said, "this was not even fifteen minutes after Ace Lindsey's daughter was last seen, and this is what the police are doing? Flirting? Checking my identification."

"What if, for Chrissake," she added, trying to get the old man to focus on the injustice of her situation, "that Syrian doctor really didn't kill the Lindsey girl? What if one of those Mexicans hanging around that place had something to do with her death? These cops would never know. They were too busy," she argued, "planning a Dunkin Donuts date to do any police work."

Dunston looked up from his coffee as if surprised to discover that Emily Goessel was still in his office. "This was the same day," he asked, "that the Lindsey girl went missing?"

"From what they said in the newspaper, she was last seen about fifteen minutes before all this. And these cops had nothing better to do than hassle me! Can you at least tell the judge?"

Dunston asked to see the video again. While he watched it, Goessel demanded that he talk with the police and threaten to turn the video over to the news media, or something.

Dunston asked if she had informed the prosecutor's office about the video? Or the doctor's defense attorney?

She had not. She had no desire to get caught up in that. She didn't have the time. She was already dealing with people who were blaming her because their kids got the measles.

"My dear lady, why are people blaming you for the measles?" Dunston asked.

"Long story short," she began, but the explanation that followed seemed to Weary Dunston to be more long than short.

"Such a travesty!" Dunston commiserated, when at last he could insert himself into the conversation again. "As a businesswoman," he added, "that is not how you want people to think of you."

"What do you mean?" Goessel demanded.

"When people think of you, do you want them to think of you as that woman—wrongly, wrongly, of course, but you know how people are—who caused those poor kids to get sick? Or do you want people to think of you as the brave woman who selflessly came forward and provided crucial evidence in the high-profile trial of a man wrongly accused of killing his beloved wife?"

This was something Goessel had not considered.

"My dear lady, your name will be mentioned in every newscast, in every newspaper. You will be, if I dare say so, the toast of the town!"

Goessel was uncertain. Her own problems were pressing; the problems of some Syrian doctor more distant.

"It is," Dunston declaimed, "after all, your civic duty. Our judicial process, Ma'am, depends on citizens like you. It is, if I may say so, just as much your duty as voting and paying taxes. More so, perhaps, because this poor man's freedom hangs in the balance!"

"You really think this is that important?"

"Absolutely, my good woman. It is a basic axiom that the Law is entitled to every man's testimony. And let's be candid, shall we? If the Law is to have every man's testimony, then so much greater must be the need for a woman's testimony. Especially, if may say so, a woman like yourself! Why Madam, your testimony is nothing less than critical if justice is to prevail in this sorry case."

"I meant," Goessel clarified, "do you really think that my testimony would be important enough to make the news?"

Weary Dunston was certain of it. She should just leave things to him.

6.

Author Note: In the trial of Rafiq A. Medawar, M.D., for the murder of his wife, Ann Lindsey Medawar, the prosecution rested on Friday afternoon. It was now Monday, and defense attorney Devin Garner was about to begin its case. *G.R.*

The bailiff stood and declared, "All rise."

Judge Benjamin Seiler entered from his chambers and climbed the stairs to the bench at his usual brisk pace. He glanced around the courtroom, taking in the surprising number of reporters and spectators present.

"Please be seated," Judge Seiler said.

"Ready for the prosecution," Assistant Prosecutor William Bradford announced.

"Ready for the defense," Devin Garner replied.

On getting the nod from Judge Seiler, Garner rose to call his first witness. But before he could announce, "The defense calls ...," he got his first surprise of the day.

At that moment, Weary Dunston burst through the doors at the rear of the courtroom, bellowing, "Your Honor! Your Honor!" The septuagenarian spieler proceeded down the center aisle of the courtroom just as fast as his spindly legs could carry him, all the while continuing to exclaim "Your Honor! Your Honor!" as often and as loud as his brittle lungs would permit.

In his wake followed a woman of some bearing, who appeared to be embarrassed, maybe even annoyed, by the commotion. Garner had no idea who she was.

Dunston was dressed in what for him was sartorial splendor. For the occasion, he wore what was undoubtedly the finest suit in his closet. Except for age and wear, it was equal in every respect to those on offer at the gentlemen's apparel stores with the deepest discounts. Judging by the suit's style, Garner figured he had been in college when Dunston bought it. But by Dunston's standards, that made the suit quite contemporary.

It was perhaps hard to tell, but Dunston had apparently even polished his shoes. True, a hole had worn its way through the sole of the right shoe. But when his shoes were firmly planted on the courthouse floor, as they were now—Dunston had stopped and was coughing violently into his pocket handkerchief—that small imperfection did not detract in any meaningful way from his over-all appearance.

Dunston's client, the woman in his wake, was dressed in a nicely-tailored and obviously expensive suit. Beneath her suit jacket, she wore a shimmering pearl-colored silk blouse. Her necklace and earrings were custom-made. Completing her outfit, the woman wore pearl-colored Manolo Blahnik pumps that went perfectly with her outfit.

In short, the woman presented herself exactly as would be expected of someone equally at ease in a corporate board room or in a social gathering in the toniest eastside neighborhood.

How old Weary Dunston came to represent such a client was a mystery to Garner. Although Dunston sometimes drew an appointment to a more serious matter, he typically practiced in traffic court, where he specialized in those cases that required the least effort. But today, the ancient litigator seemed to be exerting himself to the fullest.

"Your Honor," Dunston wheezed as he made his way past the tables reserved for trial counsel and pressed resolutely forward, "may I approach the bench?"

"Mr. Dunston," Judge Seiler responded, bemused at the ancient barrister's grand —and grandstanding— entrance. "We're in the middle of a trial here."

"Precisely, precisely," Dunston agreed, as if that had been the very point he had come to press upon the court. "I wish to address the court, if I may, in a matter of great urgency and importance. It is a matter which cannot wait, Your Honor, if the court is to avoid a serious miscarriage of justice in this proceeding."

"Fifteen-minute recess," Judge Seiler sighed. "Let's do this in chambers."

When Judge Seiler, the court reporter, counsel, and the well-dressed woman were all seated in the judge's chambers, Dunston —who remained standing— attended first to an important formality. "Your Honor, if I may," he began, "I would like to introduce my client, Ms. Emily Goessel."

The judge nodded politely in the woman's direction.

"My client has become aware, Your Honor, that the defendant in this matter, Dr. Rafiq Medawar, claims that he and a certain nurse—a modern-day Florence Nightingale, if you will – went to the Sleep Cheap Inn, on the morning in question, to care for the two desperately ill children of a woman believed to be an undocumented alien.

"It is Dr. Medawar's contention, as my client understands the situation, that this poor woman feared she would be deported if she took her children to the hospital.

"The State, on the other hand, contends that Dr. Medawar and this nurse went to this inn to attend to a very different sort of physical need. The prosecution, Your Honor, would have the jury believe that there never was a Madonna with child, hiding from the authorities—from the modern Herod, if you will—in this humble place, caring as best she could for two desperately ill children.

"On that very point rests this gentleman's honor and liberty," Dunston proclaimed, warming to his peroration. "And so, Your Honor, my client has asked me — insisted -- that she must come forward."

"Mr. Dunston," Judge Seiler chided the bombastic old barrister. "You are not addressing a joint session of Congress. Can you get to the point, please?"

"Exactly, exactly," Dunston agreed wholeheartedly. "On the morning in question, Your Honor, Ms. Goessel's own child was also ill. The child's school contacted Ms. Goessel and demanded that she come immediately and take her sick child home."

Judge Seiler cleared his throat in warning.

"As you would expect, Your Honor, Ms. Goessel left work immediately and went to pick up her ailing child."

At this point in his oration, Dunston lowered his voice and looked apologetically at his client for what he had to say next. "You might, Your Honor, say that she sped to her child's side, because — as it happened—a police officer pulled her over for speeding."

"Unfortunately, Your Honor, while Ms. Goessel may have been in too great a hurry to reach her poor, sick child, the young patrolman who pulled her over was in no hurry at all. As Ms. Goessel sat in her car, waiting for him to approach, this young patrolman and a lady cop chatted and flirted and what have you—as if Ms. Goessel and her dear, sick child had all the time in the world."

"Mr. Dunston, if don't get to the point soon," Judge Seiler threatened, "I am going to have the bailiff take you into custody and deposit your sorry old carcass next door in the Detention Center."

"Well, yes, yes, getting to the point, Your Honor. As Ms. Goessel sat there, she became frustrated, as I'm sure you would have been if the tables had been turned. In this state of high dungeon, Your Honor, my client retrieved her cell phone from her purse and began recording these two young police officers chit-chatting and romancing and what-have-you. In short, she began making a video of their flagrant neglect of their duties."

"You've got thirty seconds," Judge Seiler warned, "before I call the bailiff."

"I'm sorry, Your Honor, I have been in such a rush to get to the crux of the matter, that I have completely forgotten to mention a crucially important detail. When, in response to the patrol car's siren, Ms. Goessel pulled her vehicle over, she happened—purely by chance, Your Honor—to pull into the parking lot of the Sleep Cheap Inn there in Clifton.

"As I was saying, Your Honor, and hurrying along now, my client was making a video of these young officers chatting and flirting and delaying her from reaching her precious child. As she was doing this, Your Honor, suddenly, without warning, several foreigners walked right in front of her, between her and these young cops. Right into the picture, so to speak."

His patience exhausted, Judge Seiler turned to Ms. Goessel. "Ma'am, assuming that's why we're here, who were these people?"

"There were two men and a woman," Goessel replied crisply, "and two young—very young—children. They all appeared to be Mexican, or at least Hispanic. The two men looked tough — scary actually — and the young woman looked frightened. Because they walked right in front of me, in front of my cell phone camera, they're on the video I was making. You can see them for yourself."

Goessel produced her iPhone, opened the camera, brought up the video, and handed the phone to the jurist.

"When was this?" Judge Seiler asked.

"Friday, October 16, about 9:12 a.m.," Goessel replied. "You can see the time and date on the video."

Judge Seiler watched the video and then handed it to Bradford, who watched it and passed the cell phone to Garner.

"If I may," Dunston interjected to belabor what was now obvious. "Barely fifteen minutes after Dr. Medawar left the premises, these two desperados strong-armed this poor mother and her toddlers from the inn, and it's all right here on video."

Perhaps brought on by the powerful emotions this image stirred up, another violent coughing spell overcame Dunston.

"Your Honor," he rasped, when he could breathe again, "in view of the parties' contentions here, and given that this kind man's life, liberty and honor are in jeopardy, I think you will agree that it is imperative the jury see this video for themselves."

"Mr. Dunston," Judge Seiler inquired, "did you advise counsel you had this video?"

"No, Sir, I came directly to the Court. I didn't want to put counsel in the position of having to argue late-discovered evidence, and risk—"

"Don't you think," Judge Seiler interrupted, "that you should have contacted the Prosecutor's office and explained what your client had come forward with?"

"The Prosecutor's office? Oh, good God, no, Your Honor."

Dunston coughed again, deeply and worrisomely.

"With all due respect, Your Honor," he explained when he regained his composure, "you know how they are in that office. On the rare occasion when they happen upon evidence of real importance, their first instinct is to hide it. No telling, Your Honor, what pressure they might have brought to bear to silence my client."

"Your Honor!" Bradford objected. "There is no basis for that accusation. It's ridiculous! He owes the Prosecutor's office an apology."

"Indeed, Your Honor," Dunston responded, "now that you call my attention to the issue, I did indeed bring this to the attention of the Prosecutor's office—in traffic court. When my client appeared on the matter of her traffic citation, I explained to the young Deputy Assistant Prosecutor that my client had this video and why it was significant. Your Honor, she refused to have me send it to her. I think it could be said she did not want to come into possession of evidence that might exculpate this poor man."

"Okay," Judge Seiler persisted, "if you don't trust the Prosecutor's office, did you disclose the existence of this video to defense counsel, to Mr. Garner?"

"No, Sir, like I said, in the interests of justice, I came directly here."

"You didn't answer the thrust of my question, Mr. Dunston," Judge Seiler scolded. "If you don't trust the Prosecutor's office, why didn't you let defense counsel know what you had?"

"He's just a youngster," Dunston responded. "Your Honor, what if he were unable to convince the court that he had not been sitting on this evidence, hoping to surprise his more experienced adversary at the last moment? What then — God help us! — if the court were to exclude this important evidence? My conscience, Your Honor, could not permit me to put justice at so precarious a risk."

Judge Seiler rolled his eyes at the garrulous old goat's explanation, but turned his attention to the video's admissibility.

Five minutes later, after hearing from both counsel, Judge Seiler had his bailiff call court back into session. He then summoned Ms. Goessel to the witness stand as the court's witness. When Goessel was sworn and seated in the witness box, Judge Seiler led her through how she how came to make the video of the woman and children leaving the Sleep Cheep inn. The jury watched her video with obvious interest.

7.

Weary Dunston was pleased with his client and the dramatic impact her testimony would make. But he was not so completely focused on his client that he was unable to congratulate himself. He had, after all, every reason to feel satisfied —and not just with how things were playing out in court.

The day's dramatic turn of events in the trial would get prominent play in the evening's local news broadcasts. His name would surely be mentioned.

With that in mind, more than a month earlier, he had arranged, with what he thought to be commendable foresight, to have commercials for his practice run during the week's local news broadcasts. They would complement the news stories, he thought, just as nicely as his client's shoes complimented her outfit.

8.

Emily Goessel was making her regular Tuesday evening trip through the Wholesome Foods Store, talking on her cell phone as she pushed her cart through the aisles.

"I guess you heard," she said. "The judge let that Syrian doctor off. Maybe it's my fault. I just hope he doesn't turn around and kill somebody else. I'll hate myself if he turns out to be a terrorist or something. You just never know with those people."

"Did you hear about the kids' school?" Goessel asked. "You won't even believe this. They are going to allow some kids from China to attend the school. These kids just came into the country, fresh off the damn boat. They claim it will be a 'valuable cross-cultural experience' for all the kids."

Goessel passed on the nineteen varieties of nuts, gathered from the far reaches of the planet, and the thirteen varieties of rice.

"What I want to know is, can these kids speak English, or are they going to be holding the whole school back?"

She retrieved a package of organic, gluten-free, reduced-sodium taco shells.

"And another thing," Goessel continued. "What kind of diseases are these kids bringing with them? Ebola? That new Zika thing? Who knows what? I don't think they should allow any of them into the school unless they can guarantee they aren't bringing some disease along with them."

She opened a jar of gherkin pickles and took a bite from one. It was too bitter. She returned the rest of the pickle to the jar, replaced the lid, and put the jar back on the shelf.

"I mean, for Chrissake, that seems like the least they can do. It's bad enough we have to worry that some loser with acne is going to show up and shoot everybody."

Goessel inspected a package of salmon steaks and placed them in her cart. The package promised the salmon had been raised in fresh water lakes in Scotland, in a pollution-free and non-stressful environment.

"Oh, did I tell you that we lined up someone to do our yard this year? He's this skinny Mexican guy —looks like he can't be over sixteen, but who knows with them?"

A container of fresh Middle Eastern Parkway Hummus with Crushed Guatemalan Red and Green Peppers joined the other containers in her cart.

"God knows where Larry found him. We're not going to do a W-4 or anything. Larry had him sign a contract saying he's an independent contractor and has his own worker's compensation and liability insurance. It was a hoot! I'm sure he couldn't read a word of it."

She checked the expiration date before depositing a container of dairy-free, soy-free, unsweetened almond milk in the cart.

"The contract was in English. But I don't think this poor guy could have read it even if it had been in Mexican. Larry says that's his problem. We're not paying Social Security and every other goddam tax for some guy who bought his papers on a street corner."

A package of ocean-caught North Atlantic sardines in extra virgin olive oil, tested to assure low mercury content, dropped into her cart.

"I bet he'd sell you his sister if you asked, if you know what I mean."

Goessel selected a box of special-blend organic Bolivian quinoa with basil.

"Oh, and did you hear about Dick Warren? He lost the primary.

That surprised me. He's such an asshole, I thought he'd be perfect for Congress.

"But what surprises me more is, no one mentioned that his wife is in drug rehab again. Or, that Dick was screwing that cute little Mexican girl he has taking care of his kids."

Emily Goessel pushed her cart into the check-out lane.

"Well, listen, I'm at the checkout, and there's some Muslim girl running the register. Headscarf and everything. God only knows if she has any idea what she's doing. It just drives me crazy!"

WORKING 9/11: A Fire Lieutenant's Perspective
by Mikey Chlanda

Author Note: This story was originally published on-line by the Huffington Post in October 2016. *M.C.*

It was not a duty day for me. My ex and I woke up around eight, fed Keegan, and putzed around the house. Around ten we got ready to go downtown to check in at my restaurant, make sure everything was running ok. We had the radio on in the van as we drove downtown, trying to make sense of the news. We couldn't tell from the snippets we heard what had gone on in New York City and Washington D.C.

Johnny, the cook, looked up at us as we came in the back door at the restaurant. "Oh my God. They're attacking us!" We had no idea what he was talking about. It took him a few minutes to explain what was going on, or at least as much as he or anyone knew.

We were all speechless trying to fathom this. We had nothing to compare it to. This was how people must have felt when they heard about Pearl Harbor.

A few minutes later, my fire department radio crackled. Tones dropped for an all-call alarm, alerting everyone on the department to listen up and get ready to respond.

"Attention Miami Township Fire Rescue, please respond to your station for an all-call." Jeez, what was going on? I clicked on the radio. "Miami Lieutenant 4 responding Station 1, two minutes out."

I got to the station. All the bay doors were open, other firefighters had already shown up and were milling around. It was about the quietest I had ever seen the station, especially with so many of us there. No one was wisecracking that day.

I went to my locker and put on my gear —for once, double- and triple-checking my snaps, making sure I was ready. The chief came over and pulled me aside. "Listen, Mikey, you know what's going on, right?"

"All I know is the World Trade Center got attacked and collapsed, hundreds of brothers missing."

"Yeah, well, we don't know what we're gonna run into today. I want you to be first due today." I nodded. First due meant I would be the lieutenant in charge on 801, our first-run rig, In our fire department structure that meant I would be first command officer on every scene that day.

"K. But I gotta have Jack drive for me." Jack had been my driver for all twelve years I had been lieutenant. We had run together on the same department since 1983 and worked with each other since I joined Maples in 1978. On a day like this, I wanted someone next to me that I trusted and that knew implicitly what I would want on every scene without me having to tell him. And someone that would watch my back and was not afraid to tell me that I missed something, or that I was making the wrong choice with five guys' lives on the line.

"You got it. You want your crew too?"

I nodded.

"Alright, Rita's not here yet, but Jimmy is. You pick a couple guys to round out your crew." He went over to Dave, the other lieutenant there that was on-duty, and told him that my crew was going to bump his off. He was not a happy camper.

I picked Owen, a former Marine who had seen combat, and Dave, a volunteer who was a college professor in real life, to round out my crew. I hadn't worked with them that much, but I trusted them and I trusted their judgment.

Colin came back over to me. "He's not happy, but he knows why I did it. A-team today buddy." He hit me on the shoulder and went off to his next task.

I gathered my crew up. It was not our typical morning happy go lucky pow-wow. Everyone was quiet, looking at me. I was trying to think of what to say.

"Look, I don't know what to tell you guys. Nobody knows what's going on, or what we're gonna see out there. We already lost several hundred brothers today." We had heard about the collapse of the towers in NYC and knew hundreds of firefighters were presumed dead, anywhere from 200 to 700. No one knew what the real numbers were.

I usually started off with "Words For Today". Usually it was something safety related, something like "Be Safe Out There" or "Visors Down At All Times". The default was "We All Go Home", words that I lived by for my crew. It was my job as lieutenant to make sure we all went home –a responsibility I took very seriously.

I wondered what to say next that day.

"So today's words aren't everybody goes home, or anything else like that. I can't make that promise. A bunch of brothers are already dead. Today's words are, Do Your Fucking Job."

I looked around at the grim faces. "We all clear on what that means?" They all nodded, one by one, as I faced them in turn.

We clasped hands in the middle of our circle. "Rock n roll, guys." It was the most somber "rock n roll" I've ever said.

Nobody said a word. We broke the clasp after what seemed like an eternity to go check our rig. It was the most thorough check that 801 ever got.

Tones dropped for a run. We all froze, fearing the worst. Central Dispatch came over the air.

"Attention Miami 805, 801. You are needed for chest pain at 1816 Whitehall Drive. Miami 805, Miami 801, chest pain at 1816 Whitehall Drive."

Jack fired up 801, waiting for the air brakes to kick in. The medic unit pulled out first onto the apron, since they didn't have air brakes. We heard them go on the air "Miami 805 responding with three." They made a right coming off the station apron, sirens blaring, on the way to the scene.

801's air brake reached pressure. Jack nodded to me, but I could hear them too. I reached for the mic.

"Miami 801, responding with five to 1816 Whitehall drive on medic assist."

The cab was silent as we pulled, the muted wail of the sirens still clear through our ear protection.

I've never felt such dread on the fire department. What would normally be a run-of-the-mill run now had us all thinking, "Is this our last run?"

We pulled up to the scene behind 805, leaving enough room so that the medic crew could get the gurney out with no problem if they needed to transport.

"Miami 801, Central, on scene. Miami Lieutenant 4 establishing Whitehall Command."

"Miami Lieutenant 4 clear, establishing Whitehall Command, 801 on scene."

I sent the crew up to assist the medic unit. Jack and I sat in the front cab of 801, silent, on edge, looking around for anything unusual.

805 ending up transporting after a while. We went back to the station, silent, all feeling like we dodged a bullet, feeling relieved, but stressed, knowing we had a lot more calls to go on.

There were a fair amount of calls that day, mainly medic calls and several with people reporting odors, smoke, loud unexplained noises. Everyone was jumpy, but we had to respond to every call, not knowing what it really was.

It may get called in as chest pains, but was it really? It's well-known among first responders that a favorite tactic among suicide bombers, terrorists, and mass murderers, that there is a second wave of explosions designed to take out us, the first responders. Believe me, that weighed heavily on our minds as we responded to calls that day.

I have never had such dread responding to calls as a firefighter, or lieutenant. There were no big calls that day, just a lot of false alarms where people thought they heard or saw something. But every single call that day on the way to the scene, I thought it might be my last call.

In 29 years on the fire department, I've survived a 5-story fall, fell off a few roofs, fell through weakened floors into burning basements, and more "Holy shit, I am gonna die" calls. I was never more sure than on September 11, 2001 that I was not going home that day. The same sense of dread going out on every call sticks with me every 9/11. I've never had that feeling before or since.

And the FDNY brothers in the 9/11 documentary, taking orders, starting their way up the staircases in the World Trade Center to render assistance, did they know there was a hell of a chance they were going to die?

They were doing their job. It makes me proud to be a firefighter. We follow our passion, we believe in our mission, and we do our job.

And we do this for our brothers and sisters on the fire department. Especially the absent ones.

MY TOWER TO FREEDOM:
A Memoir
by Elle Mott

I spooned instant coffee into my cup. It was already grimy with old coffee film because it had been a few days since I last wiped it out. Luke-warm water from my plastic jug helped the grounds dissolve as I swirled it good. I grabbed a pen from my pack's side pocket and opened a day-old newspaper to scour its classified ads. I drifted into "what ifs" but was then jarred back to reality by a man's deep voice.

"Hey, anybody home in there?"

I grabbed my hammer from under my pillow. It was just behind me at the back wall, not that I ever used it, but I had to be ready for the unknown. Whoever was out there was close, and louder.

"Hello?"

I unzipped my tent and looked out. "Ya?"

"You best get to a TV or radio or something for news. We just got attacked."

I stepped out of my tent. "What?"

He backed up a foot. "Our country—Terrorist planes just flew into the Twin Towers in New York. Our country is under attack."

I dropped my hammer to the ground. "Oh no—Are you sure?"

"I just thought you should know."

He backed up another two steps then turned toward the street. I trampled my own path through the yellow grass as I followed beside him. "Tell me more."

"All I know is two airplanes got hijacked by terrorists and crashed into the Twin Towers. Both Towers. From what I saw on TV, it's bad; real bad."

I ducked from a low hanging tree branch. "The planes—how could they just crash into a building?"

"They flew right into our buildings."

Foxtails and burrs got stuck in my sandals as I walked, but I stayed close to him. "How many people died?"

"I don't know; hundreds."

We had about another forty yards to go and were still hidden from street traffic. Well, not hidden, but far enough back to go unnoticed. "What happens now?"

He shook his head as if to say no or oh no or I don't know. I didn't know what more to ask but wanted to know more. "That's awful," I said.

We were almost to the street. The tall grass was behind us and only dandelions, thistles, and hardened patches of dry dirt remained ahead. I kept up with his quick paced steps. My kindly stranger turned his head to me and said, "I have to go but you take care and get to a TV or radio like I said."

Where did he think I was going to find a TV? *I was homeless.*

I stood on the sidewalk and looked all around. Traffic was busy and not just with cars but people walked and ran too, but where to, I had no idea. I looked up at the gas station sign nearby. Its price for gas was $2.99 a gallon. This must be serious. Gas is never more than a $1.59.

I didn't know where to go or who to call. I didn't know anyone in that city. I had only stopped there for a while before going to Savannah to look for work and a place to live. I had to talk to someone, and someone other than a stranger. Sure he was nice, but frazzled, and he was no longer with me. I walked to the phone booth at the far corner of the gas station parking lot. I had change in my pocket but the only person I knew to call was Bud. It would take more than loose change to call Springfield.

I picked up the phone receiver but left my glass door open so I wouldn't miss anything important. I dialed 0 and then Bud's number, but got a busy signal which immediately preceded a recording, "All circuits are busy. Please try your call later." This must be serious.

I tried again but got the same recording. I tried a third time but still, same thing. I held tight onto the receiver. No one else needed the phone from what I could see. I stood and felt astonished. I had never seen the Twin Towers but remembered when I had seen the White House from afar when between rides. A polite well-dressed business lady had just dropped me off at her exit to work. While I had held my thumb out, a traffic cop had driven past me with a quick blast from his bullhorn "Get off the road. No hitchhiking."

At that cop's command, I had put my hand down and rested my thumb. That was years ago, and without any foreshadowing.

The phone's receiver was still close to my ear. I relaxed my arm to stare at the city commotion that moved past the gas station.

In my distant memory, I could still see that cop car. I had looked all around me but saw there was nowhere to go. I had stared at what little I could see of the Capitol Building in the far off distance of downtown Washington, D.C. It was white, the color of ivory and round; much like the round dome I had become familiar to when in Salem, Oregon. I'm sure the two are shaped a little different from each other, but I hadn't seen anything physically significant about the building that stood protecting our country. If anything, I had felt inspired by what I saw that day because it represented a gateway to our country and a symbol of freedom. I felt free on that summer day; far and free from the family who had cast me aside, far and free from the community of Salem that I came to hate, and far and free to begin life anew.

And there I stood, at the phone booth, in a new place and time but questioned how free I was. Our country was under attack. *Was I still free?*

I put the receiver back to my ear and dialed again. A live operator answered, "Your billing please?"

"Collect from—" (And I gave my name.)

"One moment please." Bud's phone rang. He answered. He accepted the charges. He sounded sober.

"It's me," I said.

Bud cleared his voice before he spoke, as was usual for him. "Hi, where are you? Are you safe?"

"Ya, I'm okay. I'm in North Little Rock. What's going on?"

"Well, you know, or I'd think you'd know, we've been having problems with Iraq. Apparently, some terrorists got on some planes and then hijacked them; two planes, and kamikazed into our Twin Towers in New York."

I looked up at the gas station sign. It was at $3.39. "Will we be okay?"

Bud cleared his voice again. "Yes, you'll be fine. Nothing is going to happen to us out here. Everything that is happening is happening on the East Coast."

"Are you sure we're safe?" I asked Bud.

"Yes. I mean the people out there aren't, but you'll be fine."

"What should I do?"

"Do you still have your radio?"

"Ya, of course," I answered.

"You can always get the 12-noon news, but with this going on, you can probably get nothing but news to tell you more. What time is it where you're at?"

"Same time as you."

Bud let out a small laugh. He always sounded like a horse neighing when he laughed. He cut his neigh short. "Yes of course, Missouruh, Arkansas. Listen to your radio. I know it's on all the TV stations here, and it should be on the radio there too."

"Okay, thanks," I said. "How are you doing?"

"I've been fine. But, you know my ma. She's going crazy in all of this, and there's no need to go crazy. Our military is good. Nothing to worry or fret over."

I knew his mom wasn't really crazy. She was likely trying to control everything again. We said our goodbyes and I promised to keep in touch. I hung up the phone receiver with a self-realization I was again on my own.

As I walked through the parking lot for my return, I looked up and saw the gas price had climbed to $4.09. A person ran past me but hesitated as he passed by. "Did you hear? The Pentagon just got attacked too." *Damn. That was new. It must be serious.*

I sat on my bed. It was a doubled sized sleeping bag rolled out flat that I slept in at night, but otherwise used as my couch and table and whatever else piece of furniture it could be to me. The floor of my tent was the same size as my bed. I had to sit Indian style as the tent stood only so high. I turned the dial on my radio and tuned it in to the public news station. The DJ said to stay tuned—I had ten minutes to wait until the President's address. I rolled a cigarette, lit it, and centered my ashtray in front of me. All I could do was sit tight and pay attention to the news as Bud had instructed of me. I wanted a stiff drink. I was not going to drink. I sat still and listened.

All I could gather from President Bush was we were going to fight back. I kept my radio on for any information I could get and pushed aside any thought that it wasn't like me to run my radio all day. I dealt myself a hand of solitaire. Cards kept my hands busy as I would otherwise have sat still into oblivion. The chunky C batteries it took cost a lot of money and so an hour of music a day was about the most it was usually turned on. This this was different. People had died and then our country locked down with high security.

When I had woken up earlier, it was with no hurry to move on to Savannah as was my goal. I knew I would get there when I got there. But in that surreal moment I felt urgency at hand. If Nana were still alive, she would have lectured me to make my bad situation good, regardless of our country's demise.

I could picture her, pure white hair pulled back in a bun and her hands on my arms to make me sit still to listen to her. "You are a strong woman. You need to let others know you need help; use their help to your advantage; make something of yourself."

I couldn't continue to live a stray life. Whether I stayed in the Little Rock area, or moved on to Savannah, I had to move forward in my life and make a life for myself. America was a land of opportunity, and the President said we were to continue with life without forgetting those who lost their lives. I had to live life to the fullest. That was the morning of Tuesday, September 11, 2001.

HOW BRIGHT EYE BECAME SKY-WULF
by L. N. Passmore

In Lisnafaer lived a besotted wulf named Bright Eye. He dared to court the grand Ladies of the Sky: Great Grian the Gold who shines by day and her younger sister Good Gealach the Silver who lights the night. So keen was he to see them rise in the sky, so hungry for their light, he pursued them day and night. His eyes shone like the first star to appear at eventide.

In their beams his grey fur turned white. Against the drifted snows of winter, all but his bright eyes and black nose disappeared. Come the green summer, his brilliant white coat dazzled all who looked upon him. Instead of chasing deer or beavers and wild hares, he sang to Grian. Being unable to choose whom he loved best, he serenaded Gealach as well.

Annoyed, the wulves told him, "If you won't hunt, shut your mouth and roll in some dirt."

He laughed and kept on calling.

He followed Grian from the moment she appeared over the Wulf Jaw Mountains in the east until she dipped down behind the Guardian Mountains on the west coast. When her slanting golden rays splashed the jagged eastern slopes of Wulf Tongue Pass, he called for her to stop.

"Just wait awhile," he pleaded. "Why such a hurry? Stay to shine your light through the tall timbers and on all the green beneath."

Grian answered, "No, Bright Eye, I must cross the sea and settle into my island bower for the night. I must not tarry. But ye may. Stay put for once. Or follow the deer. Take care to cull the old and the ill so that the trees stay hardy and your pack thrives."

He bristled and roared. The raccoons and owls who sleep during the day in dens under green leaved shrubs or in the tree tops complained to Grian. She called to him, "Hush, Bright Eye. Go find your pack. Curl that fine white tail around your noisy jaws and sleep. Ye'll be better fit for a night hunt. Make your moans to Gealach. She will light your way to a meal."

But he could not bear losing sight of Grian. He climbed to the very top of Wulf Tongue Pass to watch her settle behind the cobalt-hued island mountains in the West Sea. In her light, billowing orange-tinged crimson clouds caressed the mountain tops. Anguished sobs poured forth from Bright Eye's lovelorn heart.

Gulls, flitting through salt sea sprays that misted the rugged coast, cried in mocking screeches.

"Who ever heard, heard, heard?
Of a wulf so daft, daft, daft?
To woo Grian, Grian, Grian?"

Grian's voice crackled like pine sap popping in a fire. "Go east, harebrained wulf. The gold of day is no more. Forsake this folly. Be quiet. Hunt the silent deer." She pulled the last trailing treads of golden light within her bower.

Bright Eye refused to give up. His most lamentable howlscrossed the sea and returned to land, carried on evening breezes. Knowing the deer would protest as they foraged wildflower meadows at dusk and again at dawn, Grian tossed and turned. Storms blew over her island retreat.

Had Bright Eye stayed with his pack, they would have warned him, "Do not rile Great Grian the Gold."

When the near sky over Lisnafaer bloomed black as a wulf's nose, faint glints of light salted the far off ebon sky. Bright Eye turned tail and raced east toward the towering Wulf Jaw Mountains.

Every so often he paused, his lungs heaving. He caught his breath and then wailed—angry at Grian, angry at the dark, angry that he could not find Gealach. His fierce keens made the squirrels whine and bears grumble, "It is night. We want to sleep."

Their cries reached Gealach just as she was climbing over Marcus, the mountain north of Mount Barra where the giants live. Her silver white light poured over the snow-capped peaks, setting them aglow. This was not the first time that pleas from disgruntled beasts under her special care, ones who needed to rest under cover of night, had reached Gealach as she flew across Lisnafaer. Their harsh cries, on top of the pesky wulf's howls, distracted her. She grew cross. It was Tree Month Holly, the night before the Summer Solstice. She had hoped to spot the Holly King's return to Lisnafaer. Maybe this year she would spy him before her golden sister. "Shush, foolish wulf. Not all beasts hunt at night — as ye should. Be quiet!"

Ah, when Bright Eye saw her silver face in the lonesome sky, his happy howl sounded like water sliding over rounded rocks into a glistening pool. From one mountain top to another, from forested hills and lush glens with grasses showing silvery-black in Gealach's light, wulves on the hunt called for him to stop disrupting their attempts to fill their empty bellies. "Go home. Do some good for a change."

Deaf to their cries, Bright Eye kept following Gealach on her trip across the sky. He did not care that his paws were bleeding and his belly rumbled like an avalanche. Night after night it was the same. Soon all of Lisnafaer was in an uproar. Indeed, all the wulves chewed their paws and tails. Ravens never ceased their scolding. Then the madness spread to the deer who ran amok and bellowed out of season. No one could sleep. All were bad-tempered. Worse, the lovesick wulf threatened the Balance Green.

The light-loving Solas and dark-loving Dorcha Faer Ones, who tended the garden fortress they named Lisnafaer, debated the crisis.

The Solas said, "All life in Lisnafaer depends upon the Ladies of the Sky completing their light-giving journeys."

The Dorcha said, "They dare not stop to requite the love of a wulf."

All agreed. "Yes, something must be done."

And yet the Faer Ones, thinking surely Bright Eye would tire of his folly, hesitated to interfere with a lone, crazed wulf.

But day and night Bright Eye chased them from one mountain range to the next, back and forth. He refused to cease his amorous cries, joyful at first sighting, woeful when they vanished in the West Sea. His flesh withered; his beautiful white fur turned dull. He looked like a shaggy skeleton with eyes that glittered like heat lightning.

Finally, the Sea spoke up. "All who swim in the vast waters fear Gealach will falter and disrupt the tides. Then who knows what other dreadful calamities might follow? What if Grian fails to rise and shine?"

Their worst fears seemed to come true when, in the daily dance of the heavenly sisters, Gealach chanced to hover directly in front of Grian. Grian disappeared. Lisnafaer fell under Gealach's shadow. The day sky turned dark. High tides flooded the land. A distraught Bright Eye ran helter-skelter but never stopped wailing.

Lady Light and Lord Green, the guardian High Faer Ones of Lisnafaer, conferred. The lady dressed in a summer green gown. Star-silver clasps and emeralds, matching her eyes, decorated her snowy tresses. Around her the murky air glowed like a halo embracing a flame. Holly covered Lord Green, including the glossy crown binding his luxuriant green hair.

Taking his hand, Lady Light called to Grian and Gealach. "Hear me, my High Kin. We beseech ye. Restore order to Lisnafaer. But do no harm to the wulf, he who seeks the light, a noble quest."

From out of the gloom, Grian chastised Bright Eye.

"Your incessant howling disrupts all Lisnafaer. Your greed for our light is all out of measure. Enough of this unseemly stalking! Ye shall be sent to the black abyss, out beyond There from whence came the Faer Ones—the proper Lords of Light.

Head lowered to the ground, Bright Eye cowered. With his tail hanging like a weeping willow branch, he cried out in little cat whimpers.

Bright Eye choked and failed to breathe.

Time stood still. Darkness prevailed.

Gealach took pity on him. "Sister," she said. "The high-grasping wulf sought our light out of love and longing. His heart is pure — if foolish. We can do better for such a suitor."

She moved the width of a gnat's eyelash. Nonetheless, Bright Eye felt it and, gazing up, saw the faintest suggestion of an aura embracing Gealach, all the darker now that this golden corona had appeared. His heart leaped. Gealach moved again. The halo grew.

Grian spoke. "The kindhearted counsel of my sister and Lady Light proves wise. For your loyalty, I grant that a reward is meet and right. Ye shall stand guard in the night high over Lisnafaer, there always to see me and my sister. How like you that, Bright Eye?"

The wulf dared to lift his head. Gealach had moved on. Though still dark to his eyes, she remained a felt presence in his tender heart.

Grian revealed her full majesty. Light, like honey to the bear, fell upon the white wulf.

He gave one joyous yelp.

"Silence," said Gealach. "We weary of all the beasts crying for quiet and order."

"Yes, impulsive wulf," continued Grian. "Ye must pay the price for your heart's desire. Ye may view blessed Lisnafaer, but never leave your appointed post. Never shall ye roam the good green below."

When Bright Eye attempted to answer, Grian flared. Heat washed over the not quite contrite wulf, scorching his whiskers. She declared, "And ye shall be silent."

Bright Eye's heart sank. His tail swept the ground. At last, he nodded his agreement.

Grian recognized the goodness of the wulf. She offered him a boon. "Ye shall be our champion. It is fitting that ye be given a new name. From now on ye shall be known as Sky-Wulf."

Gealach added, "From Tree Month to Tree Month, as Lisnafaer

turns from green to white and then green once more, our light shall nourish you, fond wulf."

Sky-Wulf obeyed. Though his heart pounded, he uttered not one sound, but his eyes beamed gratitude and love.

Grian had the last word. "Sky-Wulf, your bright eye shall be a portal to the Otherworld. At times of great danger, ye may speak of what we may fail to see in the completion of our daily rounds. We pray that ye be silent until the second Great Crossing from Here back to There."

To this day, many ages after Bright Eye ascended to the heavens, all wulves of Lisnafaer know him as Sky-Wulf. If you listen, you will hear them call out to the Wulf Star to guard them on the hunt.

For additional Tales from Lisnafaer visit www.lnpassmore.com.

ALL WILL BE OKAY
by Alvena Stanfield

Before I fell asleep I'd watched "Essence of Trump" followed by "Essence of Clinton." These political foes triggered apprehensions bordering on fright. The economy, the violence, the Mexican border, the racial tension and legislators' apathy are each kindling for a national upheaval. My friend, a former college professor and published writer, summarized U.S concerns:

"This election is scaring me. Either way I'm afraid we're not too far from collapse."

While I understand candidates' brash political statements and dredging an opponent's failings permeate the media, I went to sleep believing U.S. citizens' flexibility, IQ and value systems would ultimately prevail, and all will be okay. My dreams returned me to my most okay world: our Lake Cumberland summer home when my children were small.

WHAM.

Was it the tree limb crashing onto the picnic table, the lightening flash illuminating my bedroom to 200 watts or the 80-decibel thunder? Jolted awake I looked outside. The willow's tendrils danced. The maple's limbs swayed, its leaves reminding me of pianists' fingers legato and staccato performances. Nature's symphony kept me awake until the raindrops began their soothing collage of sound. Some drops plinked against the windows. Others drummed the sill while its companions gathered, tumbling together on their way to renew the earth.

By morning, nitrogen-scent triggered by lightning's connection with the earth promises a sunny day and draws me, coffee cup in hand, toward the door. Today's news: Clinton or Trump? Trump or Clinton? escape from the TV onto the porch. Vanished emails echo Nixon's erased tapes. Failure at Bengazi echoes Kennedy's Bay of Pigs. Abrasive "You're fired;" "Your wife's afraid to speak" and "blood from…" hint of tomorrow's failed diplomacy. So many things to weigh as the nitrogen-rich atmosphere soothes. The scent of our earth renewing itself by and after last night's upheaval, gently carries a promise: "All will be okay."

Coffee cup emptied I grab a broom to sweep fallen petals and leaves. Mid-step I am stunned. Yesterday, my crepe myrtle's blooms reached upward touching my home's electric lines. Their saturated magenta puffs the size of loaves of bread rest face-down, their branches forming tall arches. In an instant, I've retreated thirty years.

"Do it again Daddy, do it again," reverberates. I see my husband wink, grin, reach upward with a hop, encircle the sapling's trunk, arms locked around it. Fanned apart his feet press against the rough bark. He folds, stretches, lunging upward, accompanied by hops firmly pressed against the trunk. I scream at him to stop, reminding him he has a family who needs him. With a grin and a shrug, he propels himself above the tree's first crotch, then the second. In one smooth motion, he throws himself toward the third branch.

I gasp. The children cheer. Legs dangling, his hands grip it. Swinging his body, hand sliding toward other hand he moves outward until the branch bends. He holds on. It bends, bends, bends lowering him to the ground. The children jump around laughing, clapping, delighted by his acrobatics.

"Do it again, Daddy. Do it again," Up he goes until the branch arches and no longer springs back.

When I lift a branch of today's crepe-myrtle arches, the rain-laden blooms sprinkle me back to reality. The children are gone. The tree is lumber. My husband rests, or rather, the cancer-shrunken and dried-by-fire remainder of him rests in a marble urn. The man who loved sunlight, life, flowers and people is too precious to share with roots and insects below.

As the sun lifts overhead, drying the blooms, the arches straighten skyward. The nitrogen-charged scent recedes and is replaced by rose and magnolia fragrances. Once again upheaval recedes and is replaced by tomorrow's promise:

All will be okay.

DOUBLECROSS: A Shaeffer Novel
by Mikey Chlanda

Author Note: The following are the opening chapters of my second Shaeffer novel, the continuing exploits of the aging heistman and his crew, which I introduced you to in my first novel, *The Heist*. My books are available on Amazon.com. *M.C.*

Chapter 1

Shaeffer kicked the door in after the third unanswered knock. He had just slipped out to get a six pack from the deli down the street —where the hell was Sheila? He dropped the beer on the hallway floor, put one hand on the Glock under his jacket, and went in. Nothing in the living room —check. Kitchen —fine.

Shaeffer went down the hallway and kicked open the bedroom door. Sheila was lying on the bed where he had left here, her head bludgeoned in with a baseball bat. The bat lay on the floor, bloodied and silent, bearing silent witness..

He spun around and strode over to the closet where the stash was. With a sinking feeling he opened the door. All three footlockers were gone. Shaeffer hurried down the hallway to check on the submachine guns when there was a heated knock on the door.

"Police." *Shit.*

"We'd like to talk to you." *Oh yeah I just bet you would.*

He shoved the Glock in the back of his pants and pulled his shirt over the bulge. Then Schaeffer opened the door to the two patrol officers. He smiled grimly and said "You guys were quick."

"Oh, you called?"

"Yeah, I just called when I saw the guy running out of my apartment when I came back from the deli. Then I came in and saw this." He pointed to the disarray in the apartment, leftovers from a hurried search.

"Mind if we take a look around?.

Fuck yeah I mind, his brain thought but Shaeffer's mouth said, "Go right ahead, put my mind at ease, check the apartment."

Shaeffer followed them around the apartment, trying to make nervous small talk like civilians did in situations like this. Hell, he had the nervous part down pat right now, but the small talk he was never good at.

Poking around, the cops getting closer and closer to that pantry door where the submachine guns were, and Shaeffer was getting nervous. The younger cop went up to the door, jiggled it and opened it. It was time to make a move.

Schaeffer took three quick steps across the kitchen and shoved the cop into the pantry. The cop went sprawling and fell down, getting tangled up in the folding chairs that were also stored in there. Shaeffer slammed the door shut, leaned against it and pulled the Glock on the older cop.

"I don't have to tell you not to be a hero. Your wife wants you home tonight." The old cop just nodded, the cold reality of the situation etched on his face.

Shaeffer bolted the lock and propped a chair against the pantry door. By this time the younger cop had extricated himself from the chairs. He was pounding on the door and yelling.

"Tell your partner what's going on – get him calmed down." The veteran cop nodded and explained the situation to his partner.

"Get your cuffs out, open them up." The cop took them off his belt and handed them to Shaeffer.

"Turn around, walk to the refrigerator. Put one cuff on, loop it through the fridge door handle." The cop followed instructions.

"Now put your feet out about three feet, and lean against the fridge with your face pressed against the freezer door. You know the drill." The cop assumed the position, not liking being on this end of it.

Shaeffer clicked the handcuffs on the old cop's other hand. Shaeffer double-checked the bolt on the pantry door and went back into the hallway towards the bedroom. He picked up another handgun and another couple of boxes of ammo. He put them in his laptop bag along with his laptop.

He took one last look around. Nothing he could do about his fingerprints in Sheila's apartment. There was no government database that had them, so it didn't much matter if they found them. Nothing to match them to.

He hurried down the staircase to the lobby and went out the front door. Shaeffer had bought a few minutes. Now what the hell was he going to do?

Chapter 2

Shaeffer was the last of the big-time heistmen. You needed a Brinks armored car knocked over or a large coin show robbed, you called Shaeffer. The problem was there were fewer and fewer large cash jobs. Shaeffer couldn't see himself robbing 7-11's to make his rent. Fuck the cashless economy.

And screw debit cards too. That was just the final nail in the coffin for guys like Shaeffer. Now nobody even carried around pocket change to pay the meter or buy a coffee. Everything was swipe swipe swipe. No angle there that Shaeffer could see.

Bad enough there were no cash payrolls anymore. Hell, nobody even got paid by check anymore. Everything was direct deposit this, electronic transfer that. What was Shaeffer supposed to do, mug some electrons?

Guys like Nolan and Parker had it made. Now those were the

golden days of cash. What the hell did they even need Brinks trucks for anymore? What were they doing, picking up electrons at the bank branches to bring to the atomic nucleus called Paypal?

This was supposed to be a dream job – a large cash haul from a one day music festival in Dayton, Ohio. No advance sales. The deal was walk-up ticket sales, but even better was the food and beer vendors. Those guys didn't take the money themselves – first you bought tickets at the organizer's booth, then you handed over the tickets to the vendor.

At the end of the festival, the vendors handed over the tickets to the organizers, and got cash for them. Less, of course, a most reasonable handling fee, of 25% for the festival organizer. 12,000 kids in attendance, say 5000 walk-up cash sales at $10 each, plus another $20 a head for beverage and food sales – a nice conservative $250 grand haul with only five guys to split.

*A quick flight in, a day or two casing the place, a few days to let the heat calm down, and we're outta ther*e. That was Shaeffer's thinking.

Shaeffer and the guys all found places to hook up so they wouldn't be any hotels or motels, no credit cards, no nothing to tie them to Dayton, Ohio.

Shaeffer bitched about the electronic world, but hey, Craigslist and Couchsurfing worked wonders when you needed a place to crash for a week or so with no questions. Not to mention all the other sites like Airbnb where people offered up their homes for a week or longer to complete strangers, no muss no fuss. It was perfect for guys like Shaeffer.

Getting hooked up with Sheila through the gypsy cab company he found via Craigslist seemed like a match made in heaven.

Big cash job, renting out a widow's spare bedroom in her apartment – what could possibly go wrong?

ABOUT THE AUTHORS

Jenny Breeden

Jenny Breeden was born and raised in Erlanger, Kentucky, and moved to Covington in 1985. She has three grandchildren. She enjoys traveling, photography, scrapbooking, and crafts such as jewelry making, crocheting, cross-stitch, and painting. A Northern Kentucky University alum, Jenny is an avid reader and considers herself a lifelong learner. She's written poetry and short stories over the years, including mysteries, historical fiction and first person narratives.

She joined the Covington Writers Group in 2014 and has been a driving force in getting its anthologies published each year. By sharing her knowledge and experience in the self-publishing world through workshops and seminars, she's helped others move forward with getting their dreams in print.

Leslie Bush

Leslie Bush has lived all her life in Covington, graduated from Holmes High School in '84 and NKU in '88 with a Bachelor's Degree in English. Her interests include Nineteenth Century British and French literature, and Fantasy and Science Fiction. She has been writing since she was eleven, and presently writes primarily in the Fantasy genre with a twisted sense of humor. She prides herself on her black humor. What can she say; she's a bloody goth. It is a world of magic and fiction. Anything is possible.

Mikey Chlanda

Mikey Chlanda is a Covington resident who was born and raised in New York City. He came to Ohio to attend Antioch College. When Maples (the college fire department) found out he had been a medic in a Manhattan emergency room, they made Chlanda join them. Chlanda fell in love with the fire service, and after college, he joined the Yellow Springs village fire department, eventually retiring as a lieutenant from Miami Township.

His first book, "Maples: A History of the Antioch College Fire Department" is a history of the only student-run fire department in the world. His other books include "The Ultimate Drummer Joke Book", "Mobile Fidelity Sound Lab", a vinyl record price guide, and "The Heist" featuring Shaeffer, an aging heist man struggling in a high-tech world. His work has appeared on ESPN.com, Huffington Post, and the Village Voice. Visit Mikey's author page at www.mikeychlanda.com and order his books from Amazon at https://www.amazon.com/Mikey-Chlanda/e/B00BHLJQH4.

Patti Kay Emerson

Patti Kay Emerson was born in September 1960 in Covington, Kentucky, where she lived until she moved to Florence, Kentucky in 2015. She graduated from Gateway Community and Technical College in 2010 with a 3.4 GPA with an Associate in Art Degree. She was also inducted into Phi Theta Kappa, an international honor society for two-year colleges.

Brad Hudepohl

R. Brad Hudepohl grew up in the western part of Cincinnati He attended Western Hills High School. He has a Bachelor of Arts in German from The Ohio State University and a Bachelor of Science in Pharmacy from the University of Cincinnati. He has worked as a pharmacist since 1976 and is currently retired.

Elle Mott

Elle Mott has embraced Northern Kentucky as her home since May 2013. Creative nonfiction writing is her niche and she joined Covington Writers Group in January 2016, at the inception of the third draft to her current big project; her life story. It is a thematic, issue-driven and high-concept personal account at 140,000+ words.

Publications include local area anthologies. Most recently, she has been accepted for two feature articles, each in a soon-upcoming issue of a national news magazine. She is a page with the Public Library of Cincinnati and Hamilton County.

Everything Elle writes is inspired by the woman who most influenced her life; her maternal great grandmother, Violet "Marie" Schmidt, nee Godsney (1904-1987). She dedicates her publications to her father, whom she came to know and love only after his death, Robert "Bob" Frank Wells (1943-2015).

Elle blogs at NovelleMott.blogspot.com and her website is http://wixsite.com/author

L. N. Passmore

As soon a she could walk, L. N. Passmore toddled into the sea. At age six she got lost in the woods, perfect for communing with tree spirits and departed ancestors. No wonder living in the Appalachians made forested mountains—filled with secret music and light—her muses. Her beloved cats, dogs, and horse became wise counselors.

She has lived, worked, and traveled all over USA, from Alaska and the Navajo Nation in Arizona to the Atlantic Coast; and the UK, from John o' Groats to Land's End. Her first of many extended trips to the Scottish Highlands brought her home to a land new to her eyes but not her soul. Visits to the western isles: Mull, Iona, Staffa, and Skye, where the veil between worlds is the thinnest, revealed the truth of Old Powers. Visit her website, Moving Mountains at: www.lnpassmore.com to read her *Tales of Appalachia*, *Tales of Lisnafaer*, and her Blog: *Mountain Musings*.

Gary Reed

Gary Reed is the author of the novels *A Fatal Cell Phone Video*, originally published as *Explicit Bias*, (2016) and *The Blockbuster Drug* (2015).

Gary grew up in Covington and attended Holy Cross for grade and high school. He wrote for edited the school's student newspaper and literary journal. Gary did his undergraduate work at Xavier University in Cincinnati, where he wrote for and edited the campus newspaper, *The Xavier News*. He obtained his law degree from the Catholic University of America in Washington, D.C.

Gary worked for as in-house counsel for Humana Inc. in Louisville, Kentucky, where he managed the team that handled the company's internal investigations and litigation. Before that, he created the legal department for ChoiceCare Health Plans, Inc. He began his career with a large law firm in Cincinnati, where he handled product liability and insurance coverage litigation in courts around the country.

Alvena Stanfield

"While I earn my upkeep by selling real estate, writing is my vacation into adventure. As an only child, I often invoked an imaginary world complete with playmates and treasure-seeking. Today there is no better escape from the chaos that comprises our world than revisiting that imaginary world. There all things are possible. If screwed up, the outcomes are easily rearranged. Take a journey with me and my writer friends into our imaginations."

Alvena Stanfield is a published author of fiction and non-fiction stories. She has recently dabbled in teaching a multi-media experience in all genres and in screen writing. She attends Northern Kentucky University and is on the Scholars List. Most recently, her interests are historic fiction set in the mid-nineteenth century western frontier. Her novel Frontier Messenger is expected to be available through Amazon early 2017.

To receive a pre-pub chapter contact 859-409-3434 or stanfieldwrites@gmail.com.

Liz Shipwash

Liz Shipwash was a member of the Covington Writers Group in 2014. She submitted her poem, Flying Solo, shortly after the editors finalized the content for Anthology 2014. Our group was saddened by Liz's sudden death on December 14, 2014. We decided to include her poem in this publication since it was inadvertently omitted from Anthology 2015. At the time of her death, she was one of the few members who wrote poetry and she would be very pleased to see so many of our current members writing it. It also makes a fitting commemoration of the second anniversary of her passing.

She was a resident of Covington, KY and a graduate of Holmes High School. She is survived by her mother, Virginia Breeden and her three precious children, Adam Carroll, Jr. (AJ), Wyatt Christopher Shipwash and Tara Morgan Shipwash, who still miss her every day.

CONTACT US

Connect with us at:

CovingtonWritersGroup@outlook.com

and

SeagullProductionsLLC.com

OTHER BOOKS
By Covington Writers Group

Anthology 2014

© Covington Writers Group, Inc., 2014.

Anthology 2015

© Covington Writers Group, Inc., 2015.

Our Traditions: A Collection of Stories with Crafts
and Recipes
from Our Members

© Covington Writers Group, Inc. in conjunction with
Seagull Productions LLC, 2016